Remarkable Women Writers

by Heather Ball

D1410130

Library and Archives Canada Cataloguing in Publication

Ball, Heather, 1978-
Remarkable women writers / by Heather Ball.

(The women's hall of fame series)
Includes bibliographical references.
ISBN 1-897187-08-4

1. Women authors--Biography--Juvenile literature.
I. Title. II. Series: Women's hall of fame series

PN471.B36 2006   j809'.89287   C2006-900182-0

Edited by Sandra Braun
Designed by Melissa Kaita
Photo research by Monica Kanellis and Melissa Kaita

Printed and bound in Canada

*Second Story Press gratefully acknowledges the support of the Ontario Arts
Council and the Canada Council for the Arts for our publishing program.
We acknowledge the financial support of the Government of Canada through
the Book Publishing Industry Development Program.*

Published by
SECOND STORY PRESS
20 Maud Street, Suite 401
Toronto, Ontario, Canada
M5V 2M5

www.secondstorypress.ca

Table of Contents

To my parents, Dawn Hayes and Roger Ball

Introduction

When I was growing up, I was lucky enough to live in a house full of books. My parents both love to read and they read to my sisters and me every night. In fact, some nights we went to bed only because of the promise of story time, and we'd always beg to hear just one more chapter. I loved the colorful language of nursery rhymes and poems, and how the stories brought me to fantastic new worlds. Then, when I was old enough, I read to myself. And I still read every day.

From being exposed to books and reading at a young age, I became interested in writing. I thought it would be great to invent characters, to share my experiences with others, and to push my imagination as far as I possibly could. Before I ever thought that I might someday write a book myself, I often wondered about how to get started. I wondered about the many writers behind the books I read. What compelled them to write?

I hope that by reading about these ten women writers, you'll learn a bit about why and how writers take up a pen and write. Sometimes, a writer's ideas come from her own experiences. She writes about her family, friends, her home, and how she feels about things that go on around her. Jane Austen loved to observe people's eccentricities, and she wrote with humor about proper society in a way that no woman had before. Louisa May Alcott's most famous book was based on her own family. Lucy Maud Montgomery used her memories of growing up on Prince Edward Island as the inspiration for her novels. When George Eliot first started writing, she used real people from the town where she grew up to create characters for her first short stories.

Sometimes, a writer wants to protest an injustice or express a strong opinion. Harriet Beecher Stowe used books to express her anti-slavery ideas. Joy Kogawa and Toni Morrison wrote because they felt the stories of the struggles of their cultural communities needed to be told. Joy wrote about the Japanese internment camps of World War II and Toni told stories from the point of view of African Americans. Judy Blume wanted to share the thoughts and feelings she had when she was an adolescent, to let young people know that they are not alone when they go through hard times growing up.

And then sometimes, a writer is compelled to write suddenly, as if she's received a gift. The first time Margaret Atwood wrote a poem, she wasn't sure where it came from, but she felt confident that she should pursue writing, even when others didn't take her seriously. J.K. Rowling was riding on a train when the idea came to her, almost out of the blue, for *Harry Potter*. Of course, ideas strike in lots of other ways, too, and all of these women have found inspiration in many different forms.

I also hope that you'll see how hard writers work. It may seem like an easy job, but the truth is that it can be very difficult. It is a slow, careful process — crafting a great story, developing believable characters, and choosing the

Introduction

perfect words to express what you mean to say. Many writers doubt themselves and their talent. They worry that they will run out of ideas. They worry that readers won't like their work or won't understand it. Thinking these thoughts is normal, but the key to success is to believe in yourself and to keep trying. All the women you will read about in this book experienced rejection when they first started out, sometimes for years. Just imagine if they'd given up, how many wonderful books the world would be missing today. Many of these women became writers in a time when most women weren't allowed to have jobs — let alone careers as writers. They defied traditional notions of what women could do in society, and they had the strength to follow their hearts and do what they loved.

Finally, I hope these stories inspire you to write something or read something, or both. Toni Morrison, the Nobel Prize-winning writer, once said: "If there is a book you really want to read but it hasn't been written yet, then you must write it." I think this is great advice. If there's something you want to write — a true story or something that came from your imagination, something funny, sad, scary, or a combination of all these things — go for it. If you don't have the urge to write, then I think that if there is a book you want to read, you should read it. So many amazing writers are out there, beyond those in this book. No matter what your age or interests, you're sure to find writers whose work you love. Ask your friends, parents, teachers, or local librarians for suggestions. You'll learn about new and wonderful people and places, identify with experiences that are similar to yours, and come to understand the lives of people who are completely different from you. Through writing you can create a whole new world, and through reading you can experience one.

Jane Austen

1775 — 1817

Some books are timeless, and even though they were written long ago, they are still enjoyed by modern readers. Jane Austen was a clever, talented writer who lived over 200 years ago. Her novels sparkle with wit and charm. She wrote about friendships, marriage, and other topics that are still relevant today, with a sense of humor we still understand. Two hundred years later, Jane Austen's novels continue to be read, loved and studied all over the English-speaking world.

Jane Austen was born on December 16, 1775, in Steventon, England. Because her father, Reverend George

Austen, was the town's pastor, the Austen family lived in the rectory, the home reserved for the church. Jane was the seventh out of eight children of George and his wife, Cassandra. The Austens loved all their children, and were especially delighted when Jane was born. They already had four boys and one daughter, also named Cassandra, and they were pleased that she would finally have a girl as a playmate.

The Austens weren't a rich family — country pastors often didn't make a lot of money and the Austens had many children to feed and clothe — but they lived comfortably. They had servants to help with chores and cooking. It must have been a very busy household where a lot of patience and energy were needed to cope with the hustle and bustle. Besides the parents, children, and servants who lived at the house, Reverend Austen often had visits from parishioners. He also made extra money as a tutor, and taught local men and boys out of his home, so his students were constantly in the house as well.

When Jane was seven years old, she was sent to school in Oxford. Her parents wouldn't normally have sent her to school at such a young age, but Cassandra was going, and Jane was so attached to her older sister that she couldn't bear the thought of being without her. The girls were best friends and one was rarely seen without the other. To describe how close the girls were, Mrs. Austen once said: "If Cassandra was going to have her head cut off, Jane would insist on sharing her fate."

Jane enjoyed school, and because she was clever, learning came fairly easily to her. When the school moved to another town nearby in late 1783, Jane and Cassandra went too. However, they didn't stay long because they both got very sick with typhus fever. Reverend and Mrs. Austen immediately made their daughters come home where they could care for them. Jane's condition in particular kept getting worse and she almost died. It was a terrifying experience for the family, but luckily she recovered after a few months.

In 1785, Jane and Cassandra went to the Abbey House School in Reading. The headmistress, Mrs. Tournelle, was very kind. The girls followed a routine of lessons and homework, and still had lots of time to play together and with the other pupils. But after only about one year, the Austens could no longer afford the girls' tuition, and had to bring them home to Steventon.

From then on, Jane was home-schooled by her parents and her oldest brother, James. Jane was lucky to be learning at home, because at the time, girls' educations were not considered important. Women weren't allowed to have careers as they do today, and were expected to marry and have children. Boys' educations, however, were considered very important because they would have careers and families to support when they grew up. Girls weren't expected to be smart, but they were expected to be genteel and refined. They had to have good conversation skills to entertain visitors and they always had to display proper manners. Jane studied languages such as English and Italian, as well as dancing and singing. Because playing the piano was thought of as an elegant skill for a woman to have, Jane learned to play, and luckily she really enjoyed it. On top of the pressure to be a proper lady and to study the arts and languages, Jane and girls like her also had to take charge of all the housekeeping duties: sewing, cooking, organizing the servants and tending the garden.

Jane was glad to be home again with her parents and brothers, because she felt the most comfortable around her family. The Austen children's favorite thing to do was put on plays, either in the living room or in the barn behind the house. With so many in the family, they practically had their own theater company. Jane also spent a lot of time reading (almost every member of the Austen family loved to read), and she especially loved to read novels. By the time she was a teenager, she had read Henry Fielding's *Tom Jones* and Samuel Richardson's *Sir Charles Grandison* so many times, she could almost recite them by heart. Reverend Austen had a huge library of 500 books, and Jane was allowed to read whatever she pleased.

Jane began to write when she was around 11 years old. She started off with comical short stories, but she also wrote some essays and, because she was quite a religious person, sometimes prayers. She also wrote short plays to perform with her brothers and sister called *The Visit* and *The Mystery*. When she began writing, it was mostly for her own amusement, or to entertain her family. She even wrote a book when she was 16 that she never tried to publish, called *A History of England, from the reign of Henry the 4th to the death of Charles the 1st, by a partial, prejudiced and ignorant Historian.* Even the book's title shows that young Jane had good sense of humor that she explored in her writing. She was a natural at seeing the funny side of everyday situations.

Jane Austen

In her early 20s, Jane became more serious about her work. The manuscripts she wrote at this time may have been first drafts of what later became famous novels. In 1795 she wrote a manuscript called *Elinor and Marianne*, which was the first version of *Sense and Sensibility*, but it was not published. In 1796, Jane completed a manuscript entitled *First Impressions* (which would become *Pride and Prejudice* many years later). She showed it to her father, who loved it. He helped her submit it to publishers, but it was rejected.

The rejection must have been quite difficult for Jane. But she was a strong person and instead of giving up on writing, she revised the manuscript to try and make it better. Rewriting the novels she'd already spent so much time on was a difficult task. But Jane was determined, and continued to rework and edit the earlier manuscripts.

A recreation of Cassandra's sketch of Jane.

Jane and Cassandra Austen took drawing lessons when they were young. Today, some of Cassandra's drawings still exist, the most important one being a sketch she did of Jane. Although we have descriptions of what Jane looked like, she never had a professional portrait done, so her sister's sketch is the closest image we have showing how Jane looked.

The first big change in Jane's life happened in 1801, when she was 25 years old. Reverend Austen retired from the church, and the family had to move out of the Steventon rectory. Jane couldn't bear the thought of leaving the only home she'd ever known, where she'd made so many happy memories. According to a letter written by Cassandra, Jane was so upset that she fainted when she heard the news.

The Austens moved to Bath. It was not an easy time for Jane, and she even stopped writing for a few years. She loved the countryside, which she describes a lot in her novels, and found the cobblestoned streets and tall narrow houses of the city very depressing. The city didn't inspire her. Bath was considered a fashionable place at the time, with lots of parties, dinners and dancing. Jane probably attended parties, but because some of the guests acted snobbishly, Jane didn't always enjoy their company. But the good thing that came out of this socializing was that it gave Jane the chance to study people, to learn about how well-to-do society behaved, so later on she could write about it with a lot of humor.

> Readers love Jane Austen's work so much that even today there are clubs dedicated to studying and appreciating her novels. The Jane Austen Society of North America, The Jane Austen Society (U.K.), and The Jane Austen Society of Australia are the largest.

Jane sold her first novel, *Susan*, to a publisher named Richard Crosby in 1803. For all her work, he paid her ten pounds (about twenty dollars), but Jane was so proud of herself she didn't care how little money she received. But for rea-

14

sons which no one ever discovered, the publisher changed his mind, put the manuscript away, and didn't publish it as he said he would. The novel was eventually released after Jane's death, making it the first novel she sold, but the last she got published. The title was also changed to *Northanger Abbey*.

When Reverend Austen passed away in 1805, Jane's mother, Jane and Cassandra couldn't afford to stay in Bath, and they moved to Southampton. Because the women didn't have careers (and Jane had not yet become a well-known author) they had no income and very little money to live on. The Austen brothers, who were married and living in their own homes, contributed money to help support their mother and sisters.

Jane's parents and brothers had always hoped that both she and Cassandra would find suitable men and get married, but neither of them ever did. The biggest reason for wanting the marriages was so that they would have husbands to take care of them, but neither Jane nor Cassandra wanted to trade their happiness for a comfortable lifestyle. Some stories say that Jane had a few different boyfriends and even a marriage proposal, but she always believed that the worst thing she could do would be to marry someone she didn't love. Jane never found the right person.

In 1809, Jane, her mother and sister moved to a cottage in Chawton. The house was owned by Edward, Jane's brother, who had been adopted by rich cousins when he was younger. He and his wife had 11 children, and Jane was thrilled to have so many nieces and nephews around, because it reminded her of the early days in Steventon. She loved being an aunt.

In Chawton, Jane felt happy. She was inspired to write again, and continued to write and revise her earlier work. She had her own room, where she could write in peace. One story says that the door to her room creaked when a person opened it, but Jane refused to let anyone oil its hinges. Whenever she heard the creak, she knew someone was coming and she could quickly hide her manuscripts from prying eyes. The cottage is still there today and has been turned into a museum. Visitors can see the small, round mahogany table where Jane worked, and the sitting room where the Austens entertained guests.

Jane settled into a routine of waking early, practising the piano, preparing breakfast and writing until lunch time. She would then take walks with her mother or do the household shopping. Because she'd always preferred the quiet life, this schedule suited Jane perfectly, and gave her lots of time to write.

In 1810, Jane submitted the manuscript for *Sense and Sensibility* to the publisher Thomas Egerton. He agreed to publish it and it came out in October 1811. The novel tells the story of two sisters, Elinor and Marianne Dashwood. One is very practical and the other is very passionate, although at the end of the book, the reader understands that the sisters are more alike than one might think. At the time, "proper" women were not supposed to write novels (it was, however, okay for men to write them) and so rather than Jane's name appearing on the book, it simply said that it was written "by a Lady." The book didn't sell a lot of copies, but Jane did make a profit of about £150 ($300). Best of all, the critics who read it agreed that it was a fine piece of writing.

> Many of Jane Austen's novels have been turned into popular movies and miniseries. About nine versions of *Pride and Prejudice,* eight versions of *Emma,* and five versions of *Sense and Sensibility* have been produced. Some have starred major Hollywood actors such as Emma Thompson and Gwyneth Paltrow.

Encouraged by her success, Jane kept working. In January of 1813, *Pride and Prejudice* (originally called *First Impressions*) was published. Again, Jane's name did not appear on the novel; it simply said it was written "by the Author of *Sense and Sensibility.*" This novel had more success than the first, and readers began to doubt that a woman could write something so smart and witty. One male writer said to Jane's brother Henry: "I should like to know who is the author, for it is much too clever to have been written by a woman."

But the author's identity was not a secret for very long. Henry was so proud of Jane that he began to tell people about his sister's work, and soon most people knew that Jane Austen was the woman behind the novels that delighted readers so much. A third novel, *Mansfield Park,* was published in early 1814.

Jane had many admirers, even the Prince Regent, who kept copies of her books at all of his houses. One of the Prince's helpers told Jane that the Prince had invited her to dedicate her next book to him. Of course, Jane knew this was really an order, not an invitation. In 1815, Jane's novel *Emma* was published with a dedication to the Prince.

Scholars believe that the dedication's clever wording shows that Jane was not completely happy about being forced to do it. It reads: "To His Royal Highness the Prince Regent, this work is, by his Royal Highness's permission, most respectfully dedicated, by His Royal Highness's dutiful and obedient humble servant, the Author."

Right after *Emma* was published, Jane knew something was wrong with her health. She felt terrible pains in her stomach and back, she had fevers, and her skin began to change color and look blotchy. Determined to keep writing, Jane began another novel called *Persuasion* and finished the first draft by 1816. She also began another novel in 1817, *Sandition*, but she had to stop because she no longer had the strength to sit up and hold the pen. Cassandra took Jane to see different doctors, hoping to find out what was wrong. Today, many scholars believe that Jane had Addison's Disease, but at the time it had no name and no cure. Jane passed away on July 18, 1817, with Cassandra by her side.

Jane Austen was only 41 years old when she died. Four months later, *Persuasion* and *Northanger Abbey* were published together. Henry, who was always so proud of Jane, wrote a biographical notice for the novels describing what a wonderful, intelligent person his sister was, so there was no longer any question about the identity of "the Author." We can only imagine what other great works Jane Austen might have written if she'd lived a longer life, but we can still enjoy the contributions to literature that she did make, which are some of the best-loved English novels ever written.

Harriet Beecher Stowe

1811 — 1896

From the time Harriet Beecher was born on June 14, 1811, in Litchfield, Connecticut, her father Lyman did not expect much from her. It wasn't because she wasn't smart, or that she wasn't willing to work hard; it was because she was a girl. Lyman was a famous preacher known for his passionate sermons, and he expected his sons to grow up and become important leaders, but he didn't think his daughter could do that. As it turned out, Harriet grew up to soar above everyone's expectations of what she could accomplish, including her own. She became a writer who helped promote freedom and justice in her country.

Harriet's mother, Roxana, was a hardworking person. She had to be, to manage the household of three girls (Catharine, Harriet, and Mary) and five boys (William, Edward, George, Henry Ward, and Charles). When Roxana died just before Harriet turned five, the children were devastated. With his wife gone, Lyman found it nearly impossible to keep up with all of Roxana's duties, care for his grieving children, and preach all at once. Two years later, he married a woman named Harriet Porter, and with two people working together, the Beechers' home life improved. Little Harriet even got two more brothers and one more sister.

Lyman had a very strong personality and he always seemed to be preaching—even at home. His voiced boomed and echoed throughout the house. And, because the Beechers were such a large family, the house was always bustling with activity. With so many children competing for attention, Harriet often felt overlooked.

To gain her father's attention, Harriet worked extra hard at everything she did with her siblings. When they picked apples, her basket was the fullest. When they fetched firewood, Harriet did it twice as quickly as the others. Lyman noticed that his daughter was special, but his best compliment to her was that she would have made a great boy.

Women didn't often have careers when Harriet was young. As a girl, her future was set: she was supposed to get married and have children. Harriet was aware of what others expected of her, but she did not like it. Harriet thought constantly about all of Lyman's talk about doing good work and leaving a mark on the world. As she tended her small vegetable garden or played fetch with her dog, Trip, she wondered how she could escape what everyone said was a girl's destiny.

One job that women were allowed to do was work as a teacher. The oldest Beecher, Catharine, inherited some of Lyman's ambition (and bossiness, Harriet thought) and opened her own school in 1823, the Hartford Female Seminary. She wanted her students to get the best education in the state. When Harriet was 12, she moved away from home to attend Catharine's school.

For the first time in her life, Harriet had privacy. She had her own room, where she spent hours and hours reading and studying. She had to spend a lot of time on school work, because her sister pushed her to achieve and made her take more classes than other students. After finishing her work, Harriet loved to paint or draw. She also started writing. In her little room, Harriet wrote her first poem, called "Cleon." But one day Catharine, who was always serious-minded, discovered that Harriet was writing for fun. She took Harriet's notebook away and gave her extra homework. Catharine thought writing for no reason, especially if you were a girl, was a waste of time.

From then on, Harriet had almost no time to herself. Catharine even assigned Harriet to teach a class when she was only 14 years old, which was the same age as many of her students. By the time she turned 18, Harriet was a full-time teacher at the school. She tried hard to feel like she was a lucky person. At least she was doing something productive and helping her students. But deep down, Harriet felt miserable. Nobody had ever asked her if she wanted to be a teacher. Nobody had ever asked her what she thought about anything. Harriet wanted desperately to make her own decisions about her own life, but her family wouldn't hear of it. She felt exhausted from always keeping her feelings bottled up.

In 1832, many of the Beechers traveled to Cincinnati, where Lyman got a position as president of the Lane Theological Seminary. Harriet was excited about the move westward, and hoped she could start over. Unfortunately, life didn't change much at all. Catharine opened a new school there, and recruited her sister as a teacher. The same old routine began again, with Catharine giving Harriet lots of extra work, such as writing a geography textbook. The book sold fairly well, but because more teachers knew Catharine's name than Harriet's, Catharine put her name first on the book as co-author, even though Harriet had written it alone.

> "When you get into a tight place and everything goes against you till it seems you could not hold on a minute longer, never give up then for that is just the place and time that the tide will turn."
> – Harriet Beecher Stowe

One bright spot in Harriet's world was the Semi Colon Club, a group to which she and Catharine belonged. Among the members were Harriet's new friends Eliza Stowe and her husband Calvin, a professor. They discussed books, art, and current events. They also wrote essays and stories to read aloud to each other. At first, Harriet was nervous to show other people her writing, but she did anyway. A newspaper editor was a member of the club, and liked one of Harriet's pieces so much, he asked to publish it. Harriet felt too shy to have her name in the paper, so the editor put Catharine's name on it instead.

Writing made Harriet happy, and she slowly gained confidence. She even entered a short story contest in *The Western Monthly* in 1834. She wrote about some of the interesting characters she remembered from growing up in Connecticut. When she discovered she'd won the fifty-dollar first prize, Harriet was thrilled. This time, her own name appeared in the paper and she was proud of it.

When Eliza Stowe died on August 6 of the same year, Harriet knew Calvin would be heartbroken. He was normally melancholy, and Harriet worried that he was not strong enough to bear the tragedy. She encouraged him to keep busy with his work, which was preparing for a series of lectures that he would give that winter. Harriet worked a lot also, and covered the lectures for the local paper. They began to spend a lot of time together talking about their work, and eventually developed a close relationship. Two years later, in 1836, they were married.

A practice in parts of the United States during Harriet's time was slavery, where Black men, women, and children were forced by white owners to work without pay, and were bought, sold, and traded like property. They had no freedom, and lived under terrible conditions, enduring beatings, starvation, and other inhumane treatment. Slavery was the biggest topic of conversation in the United States during the mid-1800s. The country was completely divided on the issue: most of the southern states wanted to keep slavery, and most of the northern states wanted to make it illegal. The state of Ohio, where Harriet lived, sided with the north, but the neighboring state, Kentucky, which was just across the Ohio River, was a slave state. Living so close to a place where people were kept as slaves, Harriet often witnessed their horrible treatment. She knew Black slaves were tortured by their white owners, husbands were sold separately from their wives, and brothers and sisters were separated. She also knew that slaves were often murdered. Harriet couldn't believe such cruelty existed in her own country, but she felt helpless. What could she, a woman and writer, do about slavery?

The citizens of Cincinnati felt the tension in the air, as pro-slavery groups argued with abolitionists, who wanted to outlaw slavery. A few times, angry mobs walked the streets, and an abolitionist owner of a newspaper had his business trashed because of the anti-slavery articles he published. Volunteers, including Harriet's brother Henry Ward, carried knives and guns to defend people against the angry mobs.

Harriet worried for her family's safety and her own, especially when she found out that she was pregnant. On September 29, 1837, she gave birth to twin girls, Eliza and Harriet, and to help her manage she hired a Black servant named Zillah. When Harriet discovered that Zillah was a slave who was hiding from her master, she knew she had to help her. Harriet arranged to have Henry Ward and Calvin take Zillah to a safe house. It was a stop on the Underground Railroad, a network of secret routes that Black slaves used to escape into Canada. The three of them had to travel in the middle of the night, worried that someone would catch them, but they made it.

Harriet Beecher Stowe

Harriet continued to think about the injustice of slavery every day, but as a wife, mother, and writer, she often felt pulled in many directions at once. As a professor, Calvin didn't make a lot of money and their family was growing. Harriet began to feel smothered by the daily routine of chores, and realized that if she kept up her writing, no matter how tired she was after a day's work, she could not only continue to do what she loved, but also earn money to help support the family. She sold many romantic short stories to women's magazines, wrote other stories about small-town life, and continued to run the household.

Several years later, Catharine came to visit, with a suggestion. Usually when her sister visited, Harriet braced herself for criticism. But instead, this time Catharine proposed that she send some of Harriet's writing to a publisher she knew in New York. When the publisher wrote to Harriet to say they wanted to make her work into a book, Harriet felt she was walking on air. Finally, she would have a real book with only her

Although Lyman Beecher didn't expect much from his daughters, other Beecher women besides Harriet made great contributions to the lives of American women. Thanks to Catharine Beecher's schools, many young women received fine educations they may not have received otherwise. Catharine's progressive ideas about education also helped promote equality in schooling for girls and boys. Isabella Beecher Hooker became a great feminist, whose views were quite radical for her time. She helped to start the New England Woman Suffrage Association, to fight for women's right to vote. She organized women's rights conventions and supported the rights of married women to own property independent of their husbands.

Harriet Beecher Stowe

name on it. She put together a collection of her stories and called it *The Mayflower*. It was published in 1843.

But the thrill didn't last long. Soon, the drudgery of everyday life started getting to Harriet again. She was bored and longed to do something big, something that society would notice. Even a move to Brunswick, Maine, didn't make her life better. By 1850, Harriet had given birth to seven children. There was something to do every minute. If she wasn't sorting out the children's arguments, she was cleaning, cooking, or trying to squeeze in some time for her writing, which was rare.

Big things were happening all across the country, things that Harriet longed to speak about and take part in. In Washington, politicians were debating the *Fugitive Slave Act*, a law that would allow slave owners to find runaway slaves and force them to return. Special officers would be assigned the job of hunting down runaway slaves and returning them to their masters. If caught, they would not get a trial or any chance to defend themselves.

Harriet Beecher Stowe

On September 12, 1850, the *Fugitive Slaves Act* became an official law. Harriet was outraged. She wrote a letter to her sister-in-law Isabella, explaining her frustration at not being able to help. Isabella wrote back to say how Harriet could help: "If I could use a pen as you can," she wrote, "I would write something that would make this whole nation feel what an accursed thing slavery is."

Unsure of how it would turn out, Harriet started to write a story about a Black slave named Tom, who had a pure heart and forgiving spirit despite his difficult life. An editor at the *National Era* offered to publish Harriet's story as a serial, meaning that it would be continued over several issues, for which he would pay her $300.

To write the story, Harriet dug into her memory of all the stories she'd heard of the ill-treatment of Black slaves. She had never been to the South, but she knew many people who had, such as Eliza Buck. Eliza was Harriet's cook in Cincinnati and was a former slave herself. The biggest influence on Harriet's story was Josiah Henson, a slave who was known for his brave escape to Canada; after he was freed, he went on to get an education and become a preacher. What surprised Harriet the most as the story came together were the strong emotions she felt. She'd always hated slavery, but in telling the story of Tom, her main character, she was overcome with feelings.

On June 5, 1851, the first part of *Uncle Tom's Cabin* was published. The response to the story was huge. Readers couldn't wait to find out what would happen to Tom next, and Harriet had to work very hard to make her deadlines. She wrote sitting at the kitchen table, crouched down on the back steps of her house, and later in a small office. As the story got longer, Harriet found a publisher to combine all the episodes into a book. The full story of *Uncle Tom's Cabin* was published on March 20, 1852.

Harriet hoped that her book would make people realize that slavery was wrong and move them to speak up about it. But she never guessed that it would cause a sensation. Six months after it came out, it had sold 150,000 copies. Word even traveled across the ocean to Europe and Asia, where the book also became a bestseller. Readers praised her for being brave enough to speak up and expose slavery as a cruel practice. But at the same time there was criticism, especially from people who lived in the South. They called her a liar. How could she know what went on in the South if she had never even been there? To prove that her story was based on real events, Harriet published *A Key to Uncle Tom's Cabin* in 1853. It is a list of all the sources she drew upon in her writing, proving she told the truth.

Harriet was an international celebrity, and she traveled to the British Isles in 1853 to share her anti-slavery ideas. Wherever she went, crowds gathered just to get a glimpse of her. People from all levels of society, from working class to well-off, knew about the famous Mrs. Beecher Stowe. Besides giving speeches, Harriet collected money for anti-slavery causes—well over $50,000 in all.

When she returned home, Harriet's desire to fight slavery was greater than ever. The tension between the North and South was coming to a crisis, and many said Harriet's book had a lot to do with it. Harriet wrote magazine articles calling on the women of the North to speak up against slavery. She also wrote another book about the subject, called *Dred*.

Division among the states of the Union grew stronger, especially around the issue of slavery. The citizens on both sides of the argument had such strong feelings that the country was splitting in two.

In June of 1860, with a presidential election near, the United States was heading toward civil war (a war within one country). Abraham Lincoln was the Republican candidate for president, calling for the abolition of slavery. Some southern states said that if he won, they would leave the Union for good. He did win, and over the next few months, seven southern states broke away, or seceded, from the rest of the country, and formed the Confederate States of America (also known as the Confederacy). In April 14, 1861, civil war broke out, between the Union and the Confederacy.

Harriet hoped that the war would not last long, but as the months passed, she worried. Many of her family members were fighting for the Union (often called the North), and it often seemed like the Confederacy (the South) was winning. Harriet wondered why President

People still read *Uncle Tom's Cabin* years after Harriet wrote it. But unfortunately, the original meaning that Harriet had in mind was sometimes changed. The book was often performed as a play, during which the lead character of Tom was made to be a clown, not the noble person Harriet wrote about. It even became an insult to call someone an "Uncle Tom." But the truth is that the original feelings behind the book were anti-slavery, no matter how some tried to change them.

Lincoln wasn't taking action. Why hadn't he freed all the slaves so they, too, could fight for freedom? Tired of waiting, Harriet went to visit President Lincoln, and told him how she felt. A famous story from this meeting is that upon seeing Harriet, Lincoln said: "So this is the little lady who made this big war?"

On January 1, 1863, Lincoln signed the Emancipation Proclamation, which freed slaves in the remaining slave states. Harriet was at a concert at the Boston Music Hall when the announcement was made, and everybody stood up and cheered. When they noticed that Harriet Beecher Stowe was present, they began to chant her name in appreciation for the big part she played in the fight against slavery. It was a huge victory for the North. Although it took another two years, the civil war ended on April 9, 1865, and the North won. By the end of the year, the Thirteenth Amendment to the Constitution officially abolished slavery in the United States.

For the next 30 years, Harriet kept writing. She wrote short stories, essays, and many more novels. Although none ever matched the success of *Uncle Tom*, people across the country and the world continued to read Harriet's work. Her career lasted about 50 years, until she passed away in 1896. Harriet's dream was always to make a difference, and she did. She rose above the notion that women could not be strong and political, and became a great writer who spoke up against injustice. Harriet Beecher Stowe went from a shy girl whose whole future was mapped out for her, to a woman who helped shape the future of an entire nation.

George Eliot
a.k.a. Mary Ann Evans

1819 — 1880

Maybe you know a person, or maybe you are a person, who is very independent. When people give opinions that are different from yours, you aren't swayed by them. You don't let what people say about you scare you away from taking a chance or trying something new. Mary Ann Evans, who was also known as George Eliot, wrote great novels that are still studied today, and she was a woman just like that. Her life was considered to be quite different from what most people accepted in the Victorian period, but she was true to herself and lived the way she felt was right.

Mary Ann was born in Warwickshire, England, on November 22, 1819. Robert Evans, her father, worked as a carpenter and went on to become a businessman in charge of supervising different types of property such as a dairy farm, a coal mine, and acres of forest. Her mother, Christiana, was often sick and stayed at home to raise the children and run the household, but she and Mary Ann were never very close.

The second daughter in the family, Mary Ann had two brothers, Robert and Isaac, and two sisters, Chrissey and Fanny. A quiet child, she often looked like she had something on her mind, and seemed to be thinking all the time. To Mary Ann, her favorite times were those she spent with her brother Isaac — they loved to fish or play marbles together — and she felt closer to him than anyone else.

When she was only five years old, Mary Ann's parents sent her to Miss Latham's boarding school. At first, she was very homesick. She cried a lot and couldn't sleep because she had nightmares. Without the comfort of her brother, she became very shy. It was hard for her to make friends or ask other girls to play with her, so to keep busy, Mary Ann began to read everything she could get her hands on. Through books, she found comfort, adventure, and amusement all in one place.

In 1828, Mary Ann finished her stay at Miss Latham's and was transferred to another boarding school run by Mrs. Wallington. By this time, Mary Ann was used to not having her family around, and she started to come out of her shell. She also gained confidence with the help of the school's governess, Maria Lewis, who saw what a smart, sensitive girl Mary Ann was. Mary Ann looked up to Maria, not only because she was a good teacher but because she actually listened to what Mary Ann had to say. A very religious woman, Maria gave Mary Ann many books to read about the subject. Although they went to church, Mary Ann's family wasn't particularly religious, but because of Maria, her beliefs got stronger. Mary Ann also learned to write and speak French and to play the piano. At 13 years old, Mary Ann transferred to another boarding school, Miss Franklin's, where her sharp mind and creativity developed even more. She even won prizes in the language classes.

In 1835, Mary Ann went back to live with her parents, but things must have felt very strange. She had gotten used to learning and studying, to being surrounded by many girls her own age, and the family home was fairly dull. When her mother died about a year later, Mary Ann wasn't sure how to feel. On one hand she was sad, but on the other hand she had never really known Christiana. As if moving home hadn't changed her life enough, suddenly Mary Ann had to take over the work of her mother and run the house. Because she was the only daughter in the family who wasn't married, she had to stay home and take care of her father, doing the chores and seeing to his every demand. In Victorian times, people thought women who were not married weren't as important as those who were, and they were especially not as important as men. Mary Ann's brothers wanted her to find a husband so she could finally be what everyone considered to be normal.

Although her housekeeping schedule was full, Mary Ann made time to keep up with her studies, to keep her mind sharp and clear. She got a tutor and learned German, Italian, Greek, and Latin. She also began to write poetry and had a religious poem published in the *Christian Observer* in 1840.

A year later, Robert retired and he and Mary Ann moved to a new house near Coventry. In the new surroundings, Mary Ann made friends with people who were interested in learning and stimulating conversation, just as she was. Caroline and Charles Bray, and Sara and Charles Hennell enjoyed talking and writing about philosophy and new ideas. They asked a lot of questions and challenged each other. Robert didn't like Mary Ann's new friends, but he couldn't do anything to keep her from seeing them.

Around this time, Mary Ann decided to give up her religion. She was most likely influenced by her new friends, who weren't religious themselves; rather than believing in God, they chose to put their faith in their own souls and spirits. Mary Ann no longer had strong feelings about church, and prayers no longer fulfilled her emotionally; she didn't believe religion was right for her anymore. Because of this, she refused to go to church with Robert. It made him angry, because he worried about what people would say if she didn't go. In the end, Mary Ann agreed to go to church with her father, as long as she could think about what she pleased during the service, and only pretend to pay attention.

Mary Ann's first work as a professional writer came about through her friend Rufa Brabant. Rufa had begun to write a translation of David Friedrich Strauss's *Life of Jesus*, but she was having difficulty with the project.

George Eliot

Because Mary Ann was so good at languages, she took over the translation. Every day for two years she worked on the book. She wanted to do the best translation possible. Even though her name was never printed on the cover and she was only paid twenty pounds for her work (about thirty-five dollars), she was proud of her accomplishment, and those who read it praised it as important work.

Robert got sick in 1846, and Mary Ann nursed him until he died in May of 1849. It was a difficult time. Robert wasn't thankful that his daughter was with him and he was very demanding. But after the three years she devoted to her father ended, Mary Ann felt lost. With a modest inheritance and trust fund to live on for a while, Mary Ann traveled to Geneva, Switzerland, to collect her thoughts and think about how she would support herself in this next stage of her life. She had already written a few articles for a local newspaper, the *Coventry Herald,* and thought maybe writing would be her career.

In 1851, she moved back to England to the big city — London. There, she rented a room from a publisher named John Chapman. He recognized Mary Ann's intelligence and asked her to work with him, which she agreed to do. Mary Ann thought up story ideas and wrote articles and editorials for John's literary journal, the *Westminster Review.* She also changed her name to Marian, because she thought it sounded more modern. People were afraid of the idea of an intelligent woman, and wouldn't accept a woman editor, no matter how excellent she was at her job, and Marian's name never appeared in the *Review.* Despite this, word spread about her work, and many people knew

During her life, Mary Ann Evans went by many different names: George Eliot, Marian Evans, and Marian Lewes.

about Marian's important role. Her reputation as a successful writer and editor grew.

By the time she was 33 years old, Marian was not yet married and her family was disappointed. It was seen as shameful to be a single woman, and people considered a woman in her 30s too old for marriage. But Marian was too caught up in her work to think about husbands. Then she met Henry Lewes, the editor of a literary journal called the *Leader*. He was already married, but his wife had been involved with another man for some time and refused to divorce him. Marian and Henry had a lot in common, admired each others' intelligence, and fell in love.

Marian and Henry traveled around Germany together, where he did research for a biography he was writing of Goethe, a German writer and philosopher. Marian continued to write articles for the *Westminster Review*. While they were both very happy with their relationship, gossip spread around London about their affair. For two people to live together and not be married was extremely scandalous at the time, and the fact that Henry was already married made it worse.

When they returned to London, everyone gossiped about their relationship. Marian got the worst of the criticism and she was cut off from society, while Henry was slightly more accepted because he was a man. Even Marian's brother Isaac, her favorite sibling, refused to speak to her, which hurt her deeply. An event Marian was scheduled to attend at a girls' college to which she donated money was canceled, and friends wouldn't come over for dinner. But Marian and Henry refused to break off their relationship because of the opinions of others.

> "People glorify all sorts of bravery except the bravery they might show on behalf of their nearest neighbors."
> — Dorothea Brooke in *Middlemarch*

Marian still published articles and reviews, but began to think more and more about writing fiction. Henry encouraged her to try, and in 1858 her first book, *Scenes from a Clerical Life*, was published. She drew on her memories of childhood and the people she had known growing up as the inspiration. Because the scandal still hadn't died down, and because Marian didn't think a woman writer would be taken as seriously as a male writer, she took on the pen name (a name that writers use instead of their real name) George Eliot. Critics and readers praised the book, but everyone thought the author was a man. The only person at the time to suggest that George Eliot might be a woman was the famous novelist Charles Dickens.

With the success of her first book, Marian was eager to keep on writing. Just one year later, *Adam Bede* was published. This time, the praise was even stronger than before. Reviewers said it was "first rate" and that George Eliot deserved a place among the "masters of the art." The next year, *Adam Bede* had already been translated into French, Dutch, German, and Hungarian, and it had sold 16,000 copies.

By this time, the name George Eliot was a famous one, especially as she continued to write and publish about one book per year. But by the time her 1860 novel,

George Eliot

The Mill on the Floss, and her 1861 novel, *Silas Marner*, were published, her secret identity was no longer a secret. Most people knew that George Eliot was a woman, and not just any woman, but Marian Evans. Scandal still existed, and readers began to criticize the novels. Some were unhappy because some of Marian's characters were women who questioned why men were always in charge, and they worried that women who read her books might feel encouraged to become more independent. Some say people were also threatened by Marian herself, who was a lot like these characters and proved that a woman could be strong and successful without depending on the approval of others. Once Marian's true identity was revealed, critics mostly continued to agree that Marian was an excellent writer, but they also began to call her one of the greatest "lady novelists" instead of simply a great novelist. They didn't think a woman deserved to be compared to a man, no matter how talented or smart she was.

To escape the criticism, Marian and Henry went to Italy. Marian wasn't discouraged at all by what others said about her, and she began researching a new novel that would take place in Italy called *Romola*, which was published in 1863.

By 1869, Marian was working very hard on what would become her greatest novel, *Middlemarch*. She was glad that her relationship with Henry was no longer such a big deal to everyone, and those who loved to gossip had grown tired of the story and began to accept the situation. Marian and Henry were seen together so often that people called her Marian Lewes, or together, the Leweses. Although she was never sure how big a role her literary fame and her money

> How did Mary Ann Evans choose her pen name? Many scholars have tried to answer this question, but no one is totally sure of the true origin of "George Eliot." Some say she chose George because it was Henry Lewes's real first name, and Eliot because she liked the way it sounded. Whatever the reason, she still felt she had to write under a man's name so her fiction would be accepted by Victorian society.

played in society's new attitude toward her, she was at least pleased that she never had to change or apologize for her choices.

In *Middlemarch*, Marian created one of her best-loved characters, Dorothea Brooke, an extremely clever, talented woman who believes women can get ahead using their intelligence. Another great character, Gwendolyn Harleth from Marian's last novel *Daniel Deronda* from 1876, is also smart and ambitious.

On November 30, 1878, Henry passed away. Marian was so full of grief that she couldn't bring herself to attend his funeral. For months, she refused to see visitors and spent most of her time alone. Eventually, she grew stronger and started a friendship with John Cross. He was a banker whose mother had died just a few days before Henry, so he and Marian had a lot to discuss. Each felt the other was a great comfort, and their relationship grew stronger. On May 6, 1880, Marian and John were married. Her new husband was 20 years younger than she was. Although some

4 Cheyne Walk in Chelsea, London, which was the home of George Eliot.

people found the age difference shocking, many, such as Isaac Evans, were simply pleased that Marian was finally a real wife. Marian didn't feel her official marriage was the most important thing. After all, she'd been committed to Henry for about 25 years without getting married. She was thrilled not only to have a companion in John, but also to be a part of a new family. John had two sisters with whom Marian got along very well, and it was especially important to her because she'd never been close with her own sisters.

Only seven months after the wedding, Marian began to experience health problems, and she died of heart failure on December 22, 1880, when she was sixty-one years old. At the time of her death, Marian was planning out another novel with a main character who was a daring woman spy. But she never got the chance to start it.

Marian Evans accomplished a lot in her lifetime. As a successful novelist, she proved that women can write just as well as men can, and that people will take you seriously if you work hard at what you do. Although she had hard times and felt lonely when people treated her poorly, she never let their attitudes change the way she lived. She believed in herself and in her right to live an unconventional life. She dared to go against what people believed was normal, and still came out on top of the literary world.

Louisa May Alcott

1832 — 1888

Some people have big dreams, such as being famous, having lots of money, or living a glamorous lifestyle. Louisa May Alcott had big dreams, but they were also very simple. She wanted to be able to help her family, who were poor and didn't have very much. She wished she could make enough money to support them. Through hard work and devotion to her family, Louisa achieved her dream and then some, becoming the author of one of the best-loved children's books of the 19th century.

Born in Germantown, Pennsylvania, on November 29, 1832, Louisa May was the second of the Alcott family's four daughters. The others were named Anna, Elizabeth, and May.

Louisa's home life was different from that of many children who lived at the time. Her parents, Abigail (Abba for short) and Amos Bronson Alcott, believed in raising their children to think for themselves. This way of thinking was unusual for the time, when many parents wanted their children to be quiet, passive, and above all obedient. Bronson and Abba didn't yell at their daughters or lecture them, but instead preferred to talk with them to explain a point of view.

The Alcotts struggled to pay their bills and were always in debt. Bronson was a philosopher and a teacher. He didn't believe he should have to work at a job he didn't enjoy, no matter how badly his family needed the money, so they didn't always have a regular income. At different times in his life, Bronson ran schools where he encouraged his students to explore their feelings and ideas — to talk instead of simply memorizing dates and facts. For one such school he moved his family to Boston in 1835. But some parents thought this wasn't a useful education for their children, and Bronson's schools usually ended up closing down.

Louisa had an adventurous spirit. Nothing scared her and she never turned down a dare. In Boston, she would go out for walks all by herself and make friends with children she met along the way. Her favorite thing to do was run as fast as she could, for as long as she could, and pretend she was as free as a wild horse or a bird.

Sometimes, when Louisa became lost in her fantasies and wasn't careful, she got into trouble. One day when she was about four years old, she slipped and fell into a frog pond. The mud was so sticky that she couldn't get up. She would have drowned if not for the actions of a quick-thinking Black man who saw her fall and rescued her. Louisa always remembered that moment, not just because she was frightened of drowning in the mud, but because the Black man was brave enough to

Louisa's father, Amos Bronson Alcott, had some ideas that people thought were pretty radical for his time. He didn't believe in eating meat and so Louisa and her sisters grew up eating mostly fruit, bread, milk, and vegetables. Because of Bronson's strong abolitionist views, the family was not allowed to wear cotton clothing, because cotton was made from slave labor. Because of his views on animal rights, the family could not wear woolen clothes either. They mostly wore clothes made from linen, which comes from flax plants.

reach out and help her. At that time in the United States, Black people did not have the freedom that white people did — many were slaves — and a Black man could get into trouble for helping (or even speaking to) a white girl. Louisa and her family were abolitionists, which means they believed that slavery should be illegal. Bronson often talked to his students about his anti-slavery views, and Abba worked with women's anti-slavery groups. Louisa felt that if the man was brave enough to save Louisa's life, how could anyone think it was right to treat him or other Black people like they were possessions? Louisa always wished she could thank him, but he left before she had the chance.

In 1840, the Alcotts moved to Concord, Massachusetts, and rented a home they called Fruitlands. They wanted to get out of the big city and live closer to their good friend, Ralph Waldo Emerson. He was a great writer and thinker, and a member of a group called the transcendentalists, who believed that people can learn more about the world by paying attention to their minds and inner spirits rather than to their senses — what they see, hear, or feel with their bodies. Louisa always remembered him as a kind person, and he often gave the Alcotts money when they had none to pay rent or buy food.

As soon as they could read and write, the Alcott girls were encouraged by their parents to keep journals. In fact, a lot of what we know about Louisa today comes from her journals, which she kept during most of her life. She wrote openly about her feelings, whether they were happy or sad. She wrote poems and stories about what inspired her. At age eight, she was so glad that winter was over she wrote a poem called "To the First Robin."

The older Louisa got, the more she understood the difficulties her mother faced every day. Abba worried constantly about how they would pay for food or firewood or how they would buy medicine if one of the children got sick. She spent all day cooking and working while Bronson lived inside his own mind, thinking about theories rather than searching for work to earn money. Louisa wished with all her heart to be rich, so she could take care of her family.

When Louisa was 13, her family moved to a house called Hillside, where she received the best gift she could imagine: she got her own room. It was tiny, with a small desk where she could sit and write. Louisa found it much easier to write in a quiet place, and she began to write more than her regular journal entries or the occasional poem.

Stories, poems, and plays poured from her pen so fast her hand could barely keep up with the ideas in her head.

The Alcott sisters performed Louisa's plays for their family and friends, and Louisa always ran the show. She chose the costumes, gave stage directions, and chose who would play which parts. Louisa never wanted to play the princess or the maiden, but often cast herself as a horse or a handsome prince, and said her lines in a deep, booming voice. The sisters started a club called the Pickwick Club (from one of their favorite books by Charles Dickens), and they published newsletters full of stories, poems, and drawings.

But Louisa didn't play all day long. In fact, she was always eager to work hard, especially when she could earn money to give to Abba. She sewed dolls' dresses, did housework, and taught lessons to local children in a makeshift schoolhouse she ran out of a barn. Louisa felt very tired most of the time, but nothing could keep her from writing whenever she had a spare minute.

In September of 1851, Louisa became a published author with her poem "Sunlight," which was printed in *Peterson's* magazine. It was published under her pen name, Flora Fairfield. The success encouraged her to write more, and to continue sending her work to magazines.

When she was 18, Louisa was offered what she thought was a great opportunity to earn money for her family. She accepted a job as a companion for a man's elderly sister, to read to her and keep her from getting lonely, but it turned out to be a horrible job. She chopped wood, scrubbed floors until her hands were red, and shoveled snow. But Lou-

Louisa May Alcott

isa refused to quit before she earned some money. She stuck it out for seven weeks and on her last day, she was paid four dollars for all her work.

Louisa thought the best way to earn money was by selling pieces she wrote. Some magazines paid five dollars for a poem or ten dollars for a story, and Louisa was determined to start making a living. Her first book, a collection of children's stories called *Flower Fables,* was published in 1854. Seeing her name printed on the cover was a huge thrill, and she earned thirty-two dollars.

While the rest of Louisa's family moved to Walpole, New Hampshire, Louisa thought she could be most useful if she lived in Boston for a while, writing and working. She wrote mostly stories with dramatic plots and sold them to magazines for up to twenty dollars each. She also worked as a teacher and was proud that she paid for her own place to live. By the time Louisa rejoined her family, her sister Lizzie was sick with scarlet fever. Lizzie did not get better and died in the spring of 1858.

The Alcotts felt stuck under a dark cloud, which lifted a bit with the happy marriage of Anna to a man named

John Pratt. Louisa was also pleased to have a short story called "Love and Self Love" published in the well-known magazine the *Atlantic Monthly* in 1860.

In 1861, it was a difficult time to live in the United States. The civil war broke out, with the northern states wanting to make slavery illegal and the southern states threatening to leave the Union if slavery was abolished. Louisa volunteered as a nurse, caring for many injured people who fought in the war.

While Louisa worked as a nurse, she came down with typhoid. Away from her family and confined to one room so she wouldn't get other people sick, Louisa felt lonely and depressed. Eventually she became so sick that her father had to bring her home, but Louisa barely recognized him because she was delirious with fever.

To treat her illness, the doctor gave Louisa a medicine called calomel. At the time, doctors thought it was a good cure for many illnesses, but they didn't know that the mercury it contained had the opposite effect, and made patients more ill. Louisa got mercury poisoning. Although she did get better, she suffered with the effects of the mercury poisoning for the rest of her life.

When she was well enough to work, Louisa began a series of short pieces called *Hospital Sketches*, which were about the different people she'd met while working as a nurse. People enjoyed the way she described each person's bravery. She also published a novel called *Moods*.

Every day, Louisa wrote to continue earning money to support her family. Sometimes she worked 14 hours a day. Abba was often sick, and they had many bills to pay. Louisa wrote many short stories, thrillers that involved mur-

Louisa wrote her first novel when she was only 17 years old, called *The Inheritance*, but it was never published in her lifetime. It was only when two researchers from Harvard University discovered a long-lost notebook among Louisa's papers that the book was discovered. It was published in 1997.

derous plots and shocking twists, because some newspapers paid up to $100 for those types of stories. But because she worried that her readers would think less of her if they knew that she was writing what was considered frivolous fiction, she published these stories under another pen name, A.M. Barnard. Louisa also began working as the editor of a magazine for children called *Merry's Museum*, and she began writing a new novel. Her publisher, Thomas Niles, suggested she write a book especially for young girls, but Louisa didn't know if she could do it. All she knew about being a girl was based on her own life, growing up with three sisters. So rather than writing a dramatic story, as she often did, Louisa began to write about her family, and based her book on things that really happened to them growing up. Her book was about a family of four sisters, Meg, Jo, Beth, and Amy, who didn't have a lot of money but who were happy to be together, despite some misadventures.

Little Women was published in 1868. Louisa didn't know if anyone would like it, but to her surprise, the first print run sold out in one month. The publisher printed more books, which sold out just as quickly. Readers wrote her letters, telling her how much they enjoyed the book, and asking Louisa to please write more about the same characters. Louisa was happy to get recognition as an author, but she was also very happy to be earning more money than before to give to her family. She promptly wrote a second part to *Little Women*, and it was published the next year.

Since the mercury poisoning, Louisa often felt tired and weak. But even when she was dizzy and aching, she continued to write. She used the royalties from *Little Women* to pay off her family's debts, but Louisa was too cautious to rely on the money from one book to support everyone. She wrote another novel called *An Old-Fashioned Girl*, and still kept up her duties for the children's magazine. Exhausted from working constantly, she decided to take a vacation.

In 1870, Louisa traveled to Europe with her sister May, and visited France, Italy, and Switzerland. Even though Louisa was on vacation, publishers and editors from her home country wrote her letters, asking her to send them stories. Now that she was a celebrity, everyone was eager to read what she would write next. *Little Men*, a sequel to *Little Women* that continued the story of Jo March who runs a school, came out in 1871.

When she returned home, Louisa had to adjust to a different life. People followed her around asking for autographs. Reporters wanted interviews. They even pestered her family. Louisa didn't like that her success as a writer took away her privacy. To get her frustrations out, Louisa wrote the novel *Work*, based on her difficult experiences trying to earn money at odd jobs to support her family.

But she was still grateful that she could now do things for her loved ones that she couldn't do before her success. She paid for May, who was always a talented artist, to travel back and forth to Europe to study painting, and she hired housekeepers for Abba, who was well cared for up until she died in 1877.

While in Europe, May married a man named Ernest Nieriker. They had a child whom they named Louisa May (or Lulu for short). Childbirth was much more difficult for women in Louisa's time, because doctors did not have the knowledge or tools they have today. May died soon after Lulu was born. Devastated by the loss of her sister, Louisa felt comforted when Lulu came to live with her in Concord.

Louisa had no children of her own, but she had spent her life taking care of people, so she wasn't at all worried about helping to raise Lulu. She spent hours playing with her and amusing her with stories, which were made into a series of books called *Lulu's Library*. The only difficulty was trying to keep up with the little girl and write at the same time, especially when she felt ill and tired. But she coped with the double responsibility and went on to publish *Jo's Boys* and *A Garland for Girls*.

Louisa May Alcott passed away on March 6, 1888. She was only 56 years old, but she had an amazing career with over 30 books and collections of short stories published. Although her body was sometimes weak, Louisa never stopped working, and stayed strong even through very sad times. When she felt like giving up, Louisa picked up her pen and kept writing. She said: "I will make a battering-ram of my head and make my way through this rough and tumble world."

Lucy Maud Montgomery

1874 – 1942

Sometimes a person's love for her homeland is so strong that it inspires her work. The name Lucy Maud Montgomery, familiar to many as the author of *Anne of Green Gables*, has always been closely associated with Prince Edward Island, where she was born. Through her writing, most of which takes place there, she made the island world famous and created a character, Anne Shirley, who became a Canadian icon.

Lucy Maud Montgomery (who always preferred to be called Maud) was born in Clifton, Prince Edward Is-

The house at Clifton where Lucy Maud Montgomery was born.

land (which is now called New London) on November 30, 1874. Her father was a sea captain named Hugh John Montgomery, who retired from his job on the water after he met Maud's mother, Clara Woolner Macneill. They ran a small general store, selling anything people in town might need, from food to buttons. Soon after Maud was born, Clara became very sick with tuberculosis, a disease of the lungs. No cure existed at the time, and Clara died when her daughter was just two years old.

Maud always had a great memory, and even as an adult swore she remembered things that happened to her when she was practically a baby. Many years later, she could still recall the day of her mother's funeral, and how sad she felt, even with her family gathered around her.

Hugh didn't want to stay on Prince Edward Island after Clara's death. Working at the store felt lonely without her. He moved away and traveled through the western provinces of Alberta and Saskatchewan, leaving Maud with her maternal grandparents on their farm in Cavendish.

Lucy Maud Montgomery

Alexander and Lucy Macneill, Maud's grandparents, were strong people. By the time Maud came to live with them they were nearly 60 years old and had already raised six children of their own (including Maud's mother, Clara) who were all grown up. The thought of starting over with a tiny girl must have been a bit overwhelming, but they loved her so much they were happy to have her.

Maud often didn't have other girls or boys to play with. Her grandparents believed in hard work, and wanted her to be serious all the time, but they knew their granddaughter was a very special child with a wonderful imagination. Maud could amuse herself for hours. She could talk for ages with her imaginary friends; to her they seemed very real. Maud made her grandparents see everyday things in a way that was fresh and exciting. She invented new names for all the trees such as Spider and Spotty, named all the flowers in the garden, and told stories about her pet cats. Maud also loved to walk in the forest or on the beach, and imagined the history of every place she explored.

Maud could lose herself in the same book for hours, and loved reading more than anything. At the age of three she could read short books all by herself and liked to read the newspaper with her grandfather. She enjoyed all kinds of stories, especially those about her ancestors. She loved to imagine what they must have been like and how they must

As a little girl Lucy Maud Montgomery was very particular about her name. She never let anyone call her Lucy and always insisted on being called Maud without an "e." This may be where she got the idea for Anne Shirley's signature request — she insisted on being Anne with an "e."

Six-year-old Lucy Maud Montgomery.

have lived. As Maud grew older, she read poems by Sir Walter Scott and plays by Shakespeare. Her grandparents had a large library and let her read what she liked.

When Maud was old enough, she started attending the local one-room schoolhouse. She was more advanced than most children in her class. Sometimes she got in trouble for talking because she was so excited to have other young people around her, she forgot to obey the rules. When she was about ten, Maud already knew she wanted to be writer. From reading poetry in school and at home, she began writing her own poems, the first of which was called "Autumn."

Maud's friends really liked her poems, and told her they admired her talent. But soon Maud wanted to reach a bigger audience, and decided, before she was even a teenager, that she would send poems to publishers. She copied her poem "Evening Dreams" onto a new sheet of paper and mailed it to a magazine. A few weeks later, Maud received a rejection letter, but she kept trying. She also began to write dramatic short stories, and was becoming recognized around town for her talent. She even won a few writing contests.

When Maud was 15, she received an unexpected letter from her father. He had remarried and had a new baby daughter named Kate. He asked Maud if she would like to come and live with them in their house in Prince Albert, Saskatchewan. It was a difficult decision, but Maud wanted to get to know her father. It was the first time she'd ever left Prince Edward Island, and she was excited for the adventure.

Right from the start, it was clear that Maud would never be completely happy with her new family. Her stepmother, Mary Ann, was pregnant and made Maud do all the chores so she could rest. Every day she gave her more work to do, and when the baby, a boy named Bruce, was born, Maud had even more household responsibilities. Cooking and cleaning didn't feed her creativity, and she ended up missing a lot of school because she had to stay home and help out. She also missed the sounds and smells of the ocean and the red sand of Prince Edward Island. It was even hard to find time to write, but Maud refused to stop doing what made her most happy.

But the best day of Maud's life came during this unhappy time in Prince Albert. She had submitted a poem called "The Legend of Cape LeForce" to a newspaper in Charlottetown called *The Patriot*, and on November 26, 1890, it was published. Maud was thrilled and proud of her accomplishment. Encouraged by her success, she kept writing, had an essay published in the local Prince Albert newspaper, and won a short story contest held by the *Montreal Witness*.

After about a year and a half of living with her father, Maud moved back to her grandparents' home in Cavendish. She was relieved to be back. She felt that her dream of becoming a writer was closer than ever, and kept writing and submitting stories to magazines across the country. She also taught piano lessons to earn extra money. Education was always important to Maud, and she missed being in school, so she decided to go back and get her teacher's license. She studied night and day for the entrance exams to Prince of Wales College in Charlottetown, and out of the 250 students who took the same exams, Maud earned the fifth-highest score.

In 1893, Maud moved to Charlottetown and was on her own for the first time. She enjoyed her courses, and worked hard to get high marks. After her first year, she had the highest marks of anyone in her classes, and she was especially proud of having the highest mark in English literature — her favorite subject. After graduation, she began to apply for teaching jobs, but it was difficult because her grandparents didn't support her desire to work. They thought women should learn how to keep house and get married. But Maud was determined to get a job and she was hired for a position in a one-room schoolhouse in Bideford, which paid about $180 a year.

Nineteen-year-old Lucy Maud Montgomery.

Maud was often worn out because she had to teach

fifty children in her class, all from different grade levels. When she was not preparing for lessons or teaching, Maud worked on her own writing. Although Maud felt she was doing a good job, she felt she would rather be the student than the teacher, and enrolled at Dalhousie College in Halifax to study literature. While there, in 1896, Maud had more stories accepted for publication, and the best part was that she actually got paid for her writing. She immediately took her money to the bookstore and spent it on volumes of her favorite poetry.

After a year of college, Maud ran out of tuition money and went back to teaching in the town of Lower Bedeque. There, she got the terrible news that her grandfather had died. Maud quit her job as soon as she could and returned to Cavendish, because she knew that her grandmother needed her. Maud immediately got a job at the local post office so they would have an income. She also wrote, and continued to submit her work. Among the many rejection letters she received, she also received occasional letters accepting her pieces, which encouraged her to keep trying.

Life was lonely in Cavendish. Maud didn't have anyone her own age to talk to, and her grandmother didn't encourage or understand Maud's desire to write. In 1901, Maud moved to Halifax to work at the *Daily Echo* as a proofreader. The editors noticed how capable Maud was, and she soon began to write her own column, about local social events and fashions, called "Around the Tea Table." She was also assigned to write parts of short stories, when the actual authors couldn't deliver their submissions on time. Soon, she began to receive more letters accepting her own stories than letters rejecting them, and her name was becoming known in parts of Canada and the United States as a promising young writer.

Maud could never have known that a single newspaper article would change her career. In 1904, she came across an article about a family who wished to adopt a young boy, but ended up with a girl by mistake. It brought back her own memories of feeling lonely when she was a child. Maud couldn't stop thinking about that story, wondering how the little girl must have felt. She began writing a short story about an unusual red-headed orphan girl who had an amazing imagination — just like her. She based parts of the story on her childhood in Cavendish. The adoptive parents in the story resembled Maud's grandparents, and Maud wrote many beautiful descriptions of PEI, so that the scenery became almost like another character in the story. In just over one year, the story had grown into an entire novel called *Anne of Green Gables*.

Carefully, Maud typed up the entire manuscript. She had to use an old typewriter on which the "w" key was broken, so she had to put all her w's in by hand. Maud sent it away to five different publishers, and after her fifth rejection letter, she reluctantly put the manuscript away. But somehow, Maud knew her character was special, and she hoped to find a publisher who felt the same way. On a cold winter's day in 1907, Maud got the manuscript out and submitted it one more time, to a publisher in the United States, L.C. Page. The following year, *Anne of Green Gables* was published and Maud was officially a novelist. The book was an instant bestseller. Even Mark Twain, the famous

Lucy Maud Montgomery

American writer, praised Maud's main character Anne Shirley as "the dearest and most lovable child in fiction since the immortal Alice [in Wonderland]." The publisher asked her to write a sequel as soon as possible. She followed up with *Anne of Avonlea* in 1909.

> Lucy Maud Montgomery wrote about 20 novels and published many more poems, essays, and short stories throughout her career. In 1943, the Historic Sites and Monuments Board of Canada declared her to be a person of National Historic Significance.

Of course, Maud didn't want to write about Anne only, and went on to publish two more books up until her grandmother died in 1911. The loss was difficult to bear, but she stayed busy with the many exciting things happening in her life, such as writing and marriage. That same year, she married the Reverend Ewan MacDonald. They spent two and a half months in Scotland on their honeymoon.

When they returned to Canada, the couple settled in Leaksdale, Ontario. Although she missed her island home, Maud felt refreshed from her trip. She had lots of ideas for new stories and the years between 1911 and 1925 were very productive for her. Still, Maud often wrote about Prince Edward Island and invented a new character named Emily who got into lots of mischief, and about whom she would write two more books. During this time, Maud became a mother and had two sons: Chester in 1912 and Stuart in 1915, to whom she was devoted.

Ewan accepted a position at a church in Norval, Ontario, and the family moved. Maud continued to write

Many people in Japan have taken a special liking to Anne of Green Gables. The book is studied in classrooms across the country, and every year thousands of Japanese tourists come to visit Prince Edward Island to see where Lucy Maud Montgomery got her inspiration.

books for young people, the type of writing she truly excelled at, but she also wrote a few novels for adults as well.

The time spent in Norval was difficult. Being the wife of a minister can be very demanding, and Maud had to help out with church duties and be an example for the congregation. Maud missed PEI desperately, but she couldn't afford the time or the money to visit very often. Ewan was often sick, and sometimes he felt depressed. Maud also missed her children, who grew up and went away to school in Toronto. The boys had inherited their mother's love of learning and education: Chester studied to become a lawyer and Stuart a doctor. But all the time Maud kept

Lucy Maud Montgomery's home in Norval, Ontario.

writing, and at this stage of her career, she never received any more rejection letters.

In 1935, Ewan retired, and he and Maud moved to Toronto, to a house Maud named Journey's End. Even in her 60s, Maud still resembled the little orphan girl Anne and

Lucy Maud Montgomery in 1932.

loved to give places poetic names. Glad to be near her sons again, Maud's spirits lifted. That same year, she received the honor of Officer of the British Empire, for all she had contributed to English literature. Although Maud often felt weak during the last years of her life, she managed to write two more books about Anne and a novel about a strong young girl called *Jane of Lantern Hill*.

Lucy Maud Montgomery passed away on April 24, 1942, and was buried in Cavendish Cemetery, which was where she had always wanted her final resting place to be. Young people and adults still read her novels today, particularly *Anne of Green Gables*, for their charm, creativity, and beautiful descriptions of Maud's beloved Prince Edward Island. Although Anne Shirley was a fictional character, she has become a Canadian icon, and her creator was one of the first women writers to put the literature of Canada on the map.

Toni Morrison

1931 –

When a child is gifted, we hope they will grow up to accomplish great things. Toni Morrison's parents and teachers knew she was very smart, and Toni worked hard to keep learning. She was one of the first in her family to go to university. But no one dreamed (not even Toni herself) that she would go on to be not only a famous spokesperson for African-American issues, but also one of the country's great authors.

When Chloe Anthony Wofford (Toni) was born on February 18, 1931, it was a difficult time in the United

States. Two years earlier, the stock market crashed and the country was plunged into the Great Depression. Many people lost their jobs and couldn't find new ones. They worried about how to feed their children or pay rent.

The Woffords had a hard time making ends meet. Toni's father, George, worked as a shipyard welder and brought home what he could. Her mother, Ramah, stayed home to raise Toni, her older sister, and her two younger brothers. Not many Black families lived in their town of Lorain, Ohio, but people of many cultures, such as Greek and Italian, lived in their neighborhood. The laws in Lorain didn't promote racism and segregation (the separation of Black people from white people), but many problems still existed. People made up their own rules. Some white shopkeepers refused to serve Black customers, and the local movie theater always seated Black people in certain seats and white people in others. Ramah was one person who ignored the rules. When she went to see a show, she sat where she liked.

The Woffords were a family of storytellers. One of their favorite things to do was to sit down together after dinner and take turns telling stories. They entertained each other this way for hours. Sometimes they told thrilling ghost stories, or adventure stories, but mostly the stories Toni heard growing up were folktales and fables passed down through generations of Black people from the American South, where her parents were both from. Music was also a big part of these evenings. They sang traditional gospel songs or songs Toni's grandparents taught them. Toni's mother sang in the church choir and had a beautiful voice. Hearing her sing was always a treat.

Toni Morrison

Because Toni was exposed to so much creativity from the time she was born, she always had a rich imagination. Whether making up her own stories or daydreaming about becoming a famous ballerina like her idol Maria Tallchief, Toni's mind was always racing. Reading was one of her favorite things to do, because with a good book it was easy to imagine you were actually in the story. When she started school, Toni was the only child in her grade one class who already knew how to read, because her parents had taught her at home.

When Toni was young, not many books had been written from the point of view of a young, African-American girl, but Toni's imagination was so great that even if what she read was different from her own experience, she still felt she understood the characters of some of her favorite authors. Many of the writers she loved came from Europe, and she especially liked classic novels. She could spend a whole day lost in the imaginary worlds of Jane Austen, Leo Tolstoy, or Fyodor Dostoyevsky.

During high school, Toni was an active student. Not only did she enjoy classes and get excellent grades, she also participated in all sorts of activities. She was class treasurer, associate editor of the yearbook, and a volunteer at the school library. Hardly anyone in Toni's family had the opportunity to go to college, but Toni was determined that she would go. She loved her family, but sometimes Lorain just felt like too small a place, and Toni craved knowledge and adventure. Her parents were proud of her ambition. They wanted Toni to use her intelligence to its full potential.

In 1949, Toni moved to Washington, DC, to attend Howard University, a very respected college with mostly Black students. She wasn't afraid to leave home; in fact, she was excited to start her new life as a young woman, and couldn't wait to learn from the professors and other students. But parts of Howard weren't exactly what Toni expected. She imagined having long discussions with classmates about literature and discovering books she'd never heard of. Instead, some of the young people she met weren't as interested in learning as Toni was. They wanted to go shopping, or to parties. Some of the girls talked a lot about meeting a man and getting married. Toni liked to have fun, but she knew she wanted to work hard as well.

It didn't really occur to Toni at this time that she

Howard University

wanted to become a writer. Although she always loved to read, she didn't put it together with her love of storytelling. But she cultivated her love of books as an English major. She also joined the campus theater group called the Howard University Players. Acting let her use her imagination to become anyone she wanted, and Toni loved being on stage with the other members of the group. They even went on performing tours.

Because Toni felt she had learned so much at Howard University, she wanted to earn an even higher level of education. After getting her bachelor's degree, she enrolled in Cornell University in Ithaca, New York, and got her master's degree in English literature. Toni decided that teaching would be a career she would enjoy, and after graduation moved to Houston, Texas, to teach English at Texas Southern University. In 1957, she accepted a position at Howard, and moved back to Washington, DC.

Although Toni wasn't an activist herself, she was very interested in the civil rights movement that was going on in the United States at the time. Even though slavery no longer existed under the law, Black citizens weren't always treated the same way as white citizens, and so they began to organize themselves, speak out, and protest. Great thinkers and speakers were leaders of the movement, such as Martin Luther King.

In 1958, Toni married Harold Morrison. He was originally from Jamaica, and worked as an architect. They tried to make their marriage work, especially because they had two children, Harold Ford (born in 1961) and Slade Kevin (born in 1964). But they didn't agree on many things,

Toni Morrison

and Toni felt that Howard tried to boss her around. Sometimes, Toni felt quite lonely. She couldn't talk to her husband and her sons were too young to understand. She was also very busy, because she kept her teaching job while she raised the boys.

She spent most of her days working, either at the university or at home, and Toni felt she deserved some fun, even if it was only for one night a week. When she heard of a local writers' group, she was eager to join. The women in the group talked and laughed. They also took turns reading stories and poems, and those listening would give comments and encouragement. That kind of setting was just what Toni enjoyed; it must have reminded her of the nights of storytelling from her childhood.

At that time, Toni hadn't written much except essays and compositions for school. At first, she read those to the group until she ran out of material. It was time to write something new. Toni sat down one night, after her sons were asleep, and began a story about a Black girl with brown eyes whose only wish was to have blue eyes. Although the members of the group liked her story, "The Bluest Eye," very much, Toni put it aside. Writing wasn't something she was about to do full time.

After her marriage ended in 1964, Toni needed a change of pace, and got a job as an editor at Random House, working on textbooks about African-American history. As a single mother living in Syracuse, Toni worked all day and only saw her children in the evenings. But after they went to bed, even if she was tired, Toni felt a strong need to write. Every night she wrote, until her short story for the writers' group became a full-length novel. She didn't expect the novel to become a bestseller, but the act of writing made her happier than anything else. Toni began submitting *The Bluest Eye* to publishers, and received many rejection letters.

Random House moved their offices to New York City, and Toni went along. She was promoted to senior editor, and worked with many famous African-American authors such as Andrew Young, Gayl Jones, and Angela Davis. Her favorite part of the job was encouraging new writers and helping them develop their work. And in 1970, Toni herself became a new writer when her first novel, which had been rejected so many times, was published. It didn't make a

As well as novels, Toni Morrison has written children's stories and a play, *Dreaming Emmett*. Based on a true event, it was written to observe Martin Luther King Jr.'s birthday, and was performed in 1986. It tells the story of a young Black man who, while visiting Mississippi, is murdered for whistling at a white woman. In the play, the young man's ghost tells the story.

lot of money, but it got great reviews and gained Toni the reputation as an expert on writing about Black cultural issues.

Like many writers, Toni worried that she would never have another idea for a novel again. However, she had no reason to fear; she wrote another novel and it was published in 1974. It was called *Sula*, and told the story of a complicated friendship between two Black women. Critics praised the novel, and soon people across the United States knew Toni's name.

She had a crazy work schedule, but Toni was used to hard work. She kept her job as editor, wrote in the evenings, raised her sons, and took on a position as guest lecturer at Yale University. But writing was what truly energized Toni, and for her next novel, *Song of Solomon*, she wrote about a male character who learns about his history and identity as an African American. The book won the National Book Critics Circle Award. Even President Jimmy Carter read the book and liked it so much, he asked Toni to sit on the National Council for the Arts. But the real rewards for Toni were more personal, such as being able to write professionally, seeing her books in bookstores, and buying a house for her and her sons on the shore of the Hudson River.

Toni and her son, Slade Morrison, have written many children's books together, such as *The Book of Mean People, The Aunt or the Grasshopper?* and *The Poppy or the Snake?*

As a celebrated author, Toni gained more confidence to express her opinions. She promoted funding for the arts and became a voice for many Black writers. In 1983, Toni left her job as an editor to focus on writing and teaching. As a professor of creative writing and African-American literature, Toni wanted to inspire young people to get excited about their writing, to love doing it as much as she did.

Many of Toni's novels explore the sad history of the way Black people were treated in the United States, particularly when slavery was legal. Her 1987 novel, *Beloved*, tells a powerful, sad story of a Black woman slave and her children, and the value of freedom. It was her biggest success yet. Toni wrote about the plight of slaves in such a way that made readers feel very deeply. Many felt it was Toni's best book, and on March 31, 1988, *Beloved* won the Pulitzer Prize for Fiction, one of the United States' highest literary honors.

The following year, Toni took a job as professor in the Council of Humanities at Princeton University, and was the first-ever African-American woman to be a chair at an Ivy League school. It was also perfect for Toni, because she got to use her expertise to help Princeton develop an excellent African-American Studies program. She also taught creative writing.

Toni often draws on a particular time in American history, such as when slavery was legal, to create a world for her characters. She went on to explore the jazz age of the 1920s in her next novel, *Jazz*. She also published a collection of essays called *Playing in the Dark*, which is about why African-

> "I can't explain inspiration. A writer is either compelled to write or not. And if I waited for inspiration I wouldn't really be a writer."
> — Toni Morrison in an interview with *Time*. January 21, 1998.

Toni Morrison was the first African-American woman to appear on the cover of *Newsweek* magazine, on March 30, 1981.

American literature is important and why it should be studied.

Because so much of Toni's work made people think about the real lives of Black Americans, and because her work is beautifully written, Toni received the Nobel Prize for Literature in 1993. The prize honors those who contribute great things to the world. Toni was the first African-American woman to win in the literature category. It was a big shock. Toni had never even imagined she'd be a writer, and she won one of the top international writing prizes. She was proud that her work had touched so many people.

Toni Morrison will probably never slow down. She still teaches at Princeton, encouraging new writers as she always has, and has published two more novels. It may seem that Toni has done it all as a writer: her work has been honored, praised, and read by millions of people. She has also raised awareness about African-American literature. She's a big influence on writers and readers all over the world. But the true rewards, for Toni, don't come from having a famous name or winning prizes – the true rewards come from the simple act of writing, from inventing worlds and sharing them with readers. Toni says that writing is something she has "no intention of living without."

Joy Kogawa

1935 —

While we may sometimes wish we had a road-map for our lives, the truth is that we don't. Unexpected events that are beyond our control affect the directions our lives take in surprising ways. Joy Kogawa's life path took many twists and turns that set her on a journey she never could have imagined. Many times, she didn't know what direction to take or what she should do. But she kept on writing and found a voice to tell a story — one that she shared with thousands of others — in a creative and rewarding way.

Joy Nozomi Nakayama was born in Vancouver, British Columbia, on June 6, 1935. Her father, Gordon, was a minister with the Anglican Church, and her mother, Lois, was a kindergarten teacher and musician. When Joy was very young, her family lived a comfortable, happy life. She had tons of books to read, and the house was always full of the sounds of music and conversation from many visitors, such as members of Gordon's congregation. They lived in a nice bungalow with a cherry tree in the backyard.

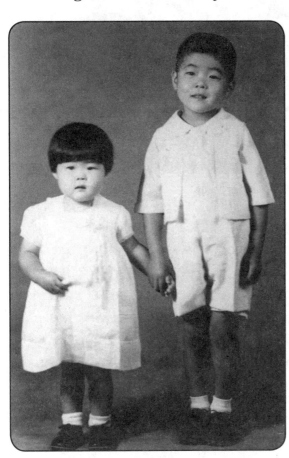

Joy and her older brother Timothy.

When Joy was a young girl, she prayed every night. She thanked God for the wonderful life she had and asked for things she wanted, and she always wanted the same two things. One was to get good marks in her classes at school; the other was to know the truth. The truth about what exactly, Joy was never sure. She simply wanted to know the reason behind everything that happened in the whole world, from the reason the sky is blue to the reason children all over the world sometimes felt happy or sad.

Joy's parents were kind, peaceful people who never yelled at her or her brother, Timothy. They wanted their children to be happy, and they didn't speak much about any problems they had. It wasn't the way of their Japanese culture to be too open about their feelings. Lois was a very elegant-looking woman, with a gentle way about her. Although she didn't always say much, all Joy had to do was look at her mother to know what she was feeling. They had a special connection that didn't need words.

In 1939, when Joy was only four years old, World War II broke out. Adolph Hitler, the German dictator, had invaded Poland and wanted to take over as many countries as possible. The world was divided into two sides: the Axis, which was mainly made up of Germany, Japan, and Italy; and the Allies, made up of the United Kingdom, the United States, the Soviet Union, and many other countries, including Canada. Millions of soldiers and civilians (people who

Japanese Canadians being relocated to camps in the interior of British Columbia.

Japanese Canadian children attending school in an internment camp.

were not fighting) died in the war. No one could have predicted the big changes this event would mean for Joy's family.

Joy was too young to understand the serious situation, and her parents, as usual, didn't talk much about it. But she probably felt the tension in Vancouver. Because Japan and Canada weren't fighting on the same side, Asian people experienced terrible racism. Many white Canadians didn't care if people of Japanese heritage were Canadian citizens just like them. Joy's parents were *Issei*, meaning they immigrated to Canada from Japan and became Canadian citizens, and Joy was *Nisei*, which means she was born in Canada, but her parents were Japanese.

During the frightening time of the war, people were very suspicious of each other. Because Japan was considered an enemy country, anyone who had Japanese roots was often seen as an enemy too, even though they had nothing to do with the war. On December 9, 1941, Japanese planes bombed Pearl Harbor in the United States. Racism against people of Japanese ancestry worsened in Canada, and the government declared them "enemy aliens." How long they had lived in Canada or even if they were born in Canada did not make any difference. The government took away their rights, their homes, and their possessions. Between March and November of 1942, about 22,000 Japanese Canadians on the West Coast were rounded up and sent away to internment camps (where they were imprisoned and not permitted to leave) and they were forced into hard labor. Even the most educated and skilled among them worked all day long in vegetable fields. Some internment camps were located in ghost towns in the Prairies and people there felt very alone. Many family members were separated from each other.

Joy's family managed to stay together, but their beautiful home in Vancouver — the only home Joy had ever known — was taken away from them in 1942. They were sent to Slocan, British Columbia, for three years. They had no choice. Then the Nakayamas were forced to move to Coaldale, Alberta. This home was a shack with only one room. They had no bathroom and the house was drafty and cold. In the middle of winter, they had to break a hole in the ice to fetch water.

In the summer, Joy and her family worked in sugar beet fields all day until they were hungry and exhausted. It made Joy sad to see her mother so tired and covered in dirt, looking very different from the elegant teacher and musician she really was. Joy longed for the days of life in Vancouver. She loved the excitement of the big city. She wished she could go back and walk through Stanley Park the way she used to, see stores decorated with Christmas lights, or ride up and down on the elevators of tall buildings.

When the war ended in 1945, the Canadian government didn't give the Japanese Canadians back their freedoms right away, and the rules restricting where they could live and what they could do stayed in place until 1949. It was difficult, but Joy's family did their best to pick up the pieces of their lives and move on. Again, they didn't discuss what had happened to them. They wanted to forget about it and rebuild the lives they had lost.

When she was 19 years old, Joy worked as a teacher in Coaldale, but she had so many bad memories there she didn't want to stay. Instead, she applied and was accepted to the University of Toronto, where she studied music (which she loved because of her mother's influence) and religion (which she loved because of her father's influence).

In 1956 Joy was living in Vancouver, where she met and married David Kogawa. In the next few years, they had a son named Gordon and a daughter named Deidre. By 1960, Joy couldn't work outside of her home because she had two small children to care for. She felt an urge to do something creative, and although music was her first love, she began to write. Joy didn't know if she would be any good at it, or if it was the right thing to do, but it felt right, and she trusted herself to at least give it a try. Whenever she had a quiet moment, Joy picked up a pen and wrote poems or stories.

To start off, Joy submitted short stories and poems to any magazine she could think of. She received lots of rejection letters at first, but she kept trying. Also, Joy hadn't yet discovered what direction she would take as a writer. She hadn't read much, if anything, by Japanese writers, or stories with Japanese characters. Her mother had told her old Japanese folktales when she was little, but that was Joy's only experience of Asian literature.

Joy has been honored for both her writing and her activism. She was made a member of the Order of Canada in 1986. In 2001, she received a Lifetime Achievement Award from the Association of Asian American Studies and the NAJC Award from the National Association of Japanese Canadians.

Joy first got published in 1964, with her short story, "Are There Any Shoes in Heaven?" In the story, a family leaves British Columbia and moves to

Joy Kogawa

Alberta, and the main character is unhappy in his new home. Although the family in Joy's story is white and the main character is a boy, it is very similar to what happened to Joy as a child. But Joy didn't think anyone would want to read the story if she told it from her own point of view, that of a Japanese Canadian.

Meanwhile, Joy's talent for poetry blossomed. She drew on her dreams for inspiration and wrote them down as soon as she woke up. She then wrote poems based on her dreams. Joy submitted her work to literary magazines, and published a collection of poetry in 1967 called *The Splintered Moon*. The following year, Joy and her husband divorced. The break-up of a family is never easy, and Joy's poetry must have helped her work through her feelings. She became a well-known poet with other books, such as *A Choice of Dreams* and *Jericho Road*.

From 1974 to 1976, Joy worked as a staff writer at the office of Prime Minister Pierre Trudeau in Ottawa. From the success of her books of poetry, Joy's reputation as an excellent poet grew, and she held the job of writer in residence at the University of Ottawa in 1978. Joy's natural tendency was to write mostly poetry, but she began to think about writing more prose. It was around this time that she had the idea to write a story based on her experiences in the internment camps as a child. She was especially encouraged after taking a trip to California to meet with Asian American writers. They wrote in the voices of their culture, and so Joy decided to write "Obasan" (which means aunt in Japanese), not for political reasons, but because the story burned inside of her to be told. It started off as a short story (published in *Canadian Forum* in 1978), but Joy felt there was more to tell than she could fit on only a few pages.

Joy began to research the history of Japanese Canadians, searching through stacks of old papers and photographs at the National Archives in Ottawa. She had heard of a woman named Muriel Kitagawa, a Japanese Canadian who lived in Vancouver during the war. Muriel, who had died in 1974, had written many letters to her brother in Toronto, describing the tension on the West Coast. One night, Joy had a dream telling her that she must read Muriel's letters. At first she didn't know if she should take her dream seriously, but she trusted her instinct, and found the letters, which were kept at the National Archives. Reading Muriel's story brought back many memories for Joy and she set to work on turning "Obasan" into a full-length novel. She felt as though Muriel's spirit was somehow working through her. Joy even modeled a character, Emily, after what she knew of Muriel. The novel's narrator is a girl named Naomi, who is a lot like young Joy, and the story traces what happened to her during the Japanese internment of World War II and how it affected her throughout her life.

Obasan was published as a novel in 1981. Immediately readers recognized it not only as a beautifully written book, but as an important account of a dark time in Canadian history. The novel won the Canadian Authors Association Book of the Year Award and an award for best first novel from *Books in Canada*. *Obasan* helped educate people about the truth of the way 22,000 people were treated, and it was one of the first books in Canada to tackle the subject. It also sparked a realization in the Japanese Canadian community. They had never received any compensation for what had happened to them. They had never demanded or received an apology. To help educate those who weren't around during war time, Joy also wrote a version of the novel for children called *Naomi's Road*, which came out in 1986.

Joy didn't know how much writing the novel would affect her life, or that the path of her life would change direction because of it. Joy became heavily involved in the redress movement — activists for Japanese Canadians pressured the government for an apology and compensation, to try to make amends for the horrible way they were treated during the war. Joy believed the right thing to do was to make public the real story of what happened to her and others like her in the internment camps. Joy worked with the National Association of Japanese Canadians, and lobbied the government for compensation for all the people whose lives were taken away. On September 22, 1988, Prime Minister Brian Mulroney signed the Redress Agreement, which promised $21,000 to every Japanese Canadian who had suffered because of the government's actions. The government also gave a formal apology. It was a huge victory for Joy and the Japanese-Canadian community.

When Joy was more able to focus on writing, she wrote a sequel to *Obasan* called *Itsuka*. She used her life as inspiration for her work. The novel follows her character Naomi through the redress movement, in a way similar to Joy's experience. Her third novel, *The Rain Ascends*, was published in 1995. Joy also continued to write

In 2005, the Vancouver Opera Company began touring schools and community centers with a stage version of *Naomi's Road*.

poetry, such as *A Song of Lilith*, which came out in 2000 — a book that is one long poem. It tells the story of Lilith, a character from the Bible, who some believe was created as an equal to Adam, but was banished from the garden of Eden for being too strong-willed.

When Joy was in Vancouver in 2003, she went back to her first house. Even though she and her family were forced out when Joy was only six, she always kept a mental picture of the home on West 64th Avenue. Joy was surprised to see that the house was up for sale. She imagined what it would be like if she could buy the house herself, but she could not possibly afford it. Because the house was getting old, Joy worried that whoever bought the house would want to tear it down.

Once word spread that Joy's old house might be in trouble, people got together and formed a group called the Save the Kogawa House Committee. They continue to hold events to raise awareness about why the house represents an important part of Canada's history, and would like the home to be designated as a historic site so it can never be torn down or changed.

"[Writing is] like a compulsion without really knowing what results from it, except if I don't do it, it feels like I'll collapse. In writing I keep breathing, I keep living, and it feels so good when I've got that right word out."
— Joy Kogawa in an interview with Janice Williamson

Joy lives mostly in Toronto, but also spends a lot of time in Vancouver. She continues to write, and to trust that the path of her life will always take her in the right direction. With her successful novels, poetry, and political activism, it has certainly guided her well so far.

Judy Blume

1938 –

G rowing up can be difficult, especially during the times when you feel like no one understands you. Everybody needs someone with whom they can talk and ask questions. Judy Blume remembers exactly what it was like to feel all sorts of confusing emotions when she was a girl. She kept her feelings inside and had a lot of questions that went unanswered. When she became an author of books for young people, Judy wanted readers to know that they aren't alone when they feel bad. Her characters are regular children who experience the same things you do. She writes honestly about what it's like to grow up, and even though it has gotten her into trouble, generations of children admire her openness.

Judy Sussman was born in Elizabeth, New Jersey, on February 12, 1938. Her father, Rudolph, was a dentist, and her mother, Esther, stayed home to raise Judy and her older brother, David.

As a child, Judy spent a lot of time daydreaming about what she wanted to be when she grew up. She loved books and was always reading something. In the 1940s, people listened to stories on the radio. (The television was still quite a new invention, and most people didn't have TV in their homes.) Judy and her family would sit in front of the radio and listen to stories about detectives solving mysteries, or spies gathering secret information. Judy imagined she might have a glamorous career like the main characters, or maybe she would be a dancer like her favorite movie star, Margaret O'Brien.

While she bounced a ball, while she played with her dolls, and while she practised the piano, Judy was always making up stories in her head. But because she was shy, she never told them to anybody. What if people thought she was weird?

Judy was also very sensitive. Her mother used to tease her by saying: "We never have to punish Judy. All we have to do is look at her the wrong way and she'll cry." Judy couldn't talk to her parents when she was upset. She thought that if she told them what she really felt when she was angry or confused, they would think there was something wrong with her. She even bottled up her nervousness when her parents announced that Esther, David, and Judy were moving from Elizabeth to Miami Beach, Florida, for a year. David was sick with a kidney infection, and the doctor thought it best that he live in a warmer climate for a while. Rudolph had to stay behind to run his dental practice. Judy was about to start grade three, and worried that it would be hard to make new friends.

But Judy liked her new school and new home. She made friends quickly. Together they swam in the ocean, rode their bicycles around the neighborhood, and played hopscotch. One of the best times was when Judy and her friends put on a dance show for their parents. They made up the dances, created costumes, and had lots of fun pretending to be professional ballet dancers.

After the school year was over, the three Sussmans moved back to New Jersey for the summer. They returned to Florida the next fall, and at the end of that school year, went back to New Jersey for good. Moving didn't bother Judy as much as it did the first time, because making friends had given her confidence. The older she got, the more outgoing she became. By the time Judy was a teenager, she was brave enough to go away to camp alone for the whole summer. Most years at camp she had a great time, except the summer when she was 15. Esther called to tell Judy that her grandmother had died. It was all Judy could think about for the rest of her stay at camp. When she got home, she didn't feel comfortable telling her parents how sad she felt, and pretended everything was fine. She was afraid they wouldn't understand her feelings.

Throughout high school, Judy kept herself very busy. Battin High School was an all-girls school, so she never had to deal with any sexism from teachers or other students. Nobody told the girls that they couldn't do everything boys could do. Not only was Judy an excellent student, but she also worked on the school newspaper writing articles, sang in the school choir, and performed in dance recitals.

After graduating with honors, Judy went to Boston University to become a teacher. Unfortunately, before she could get used to her new life, Judy got very sick with mononucleosis (which causes a person to feel exhausted and run a fever, often for months) and she had to go home to get well.

When she recovered, Judy was ready to continue with her schooling, and this time she enrolled in New York University as an education major. There she met a man named John Blume, and they got married. Although the wedding was supposed to be a happy event, Judy's father died suddenly of a heart attack just before the big day, making it impossible to feel cheerful. His death cast a sad shadow on Judy's first year of marriage, but she distracted herself by studying very hard so she could graduate university.

In 1961, Judy had a daughter she named Randy, and in 1963 she had a son named Larry. She didn't have time to start teaching because the next few years were busy ones. As a mother, Judy always had responsibilities, such as making the children's lunches or driving them to a friend's house. Although she had a nice house and a nice family, deep in her heart Judy wasn't happy. Something was missing from her life, but she didn't know what it was.

Judy Blume

Judy came up with an idea to try to fill the hole in her life. She turned to what she had always loved as a child: stories. Nobody knew about the stories she used make up as a young girl, and nobody knew that she had continued to make up stories as an adult. But now she would write them down. Feeling excited, she began to write children's stories, hoping that she could get them published. She sent what she wrote to magazines and book publishers, but success wasn't as simple as she'd thought. When she received her first rejection letters, Judy cried. It made her want to give up writing. But she dried her tears and sent out more stories. Soon, she was receiving up to six rejection letters a week. Still, she kept trying.

One day, Judy received a flyer for a writing class at New York University, where students learned to write stories for children and young adults. She signed up right away. Being in school again was wonderful because she loved learning about the craft of writing. In fact, she found the class so helpful she took it twice.

Judy's first book was published in 1969, called *The One in the Middle is the Green Kangaroo*. She was only 27 years old. When she got the news of her book's acceptance, Judy danced around the house with excitement. Her husband was happy for her, but Judy knew he didn't take her work seriously. He thought writing wasn't real work and that because she wasn't making a lot of money, it wasn't worth her time. Judy didn't share his opinion.

Richard Jackson was a young publisher who was looking to take a chance on new writers. He read some of Judy's work, and they had a meeting to talk about what she could improve on. He wanted to know many important things, such as why a certain character said something, or what a character was feeling. He encouraged Judy to treat her characters like real people and to make her stories as realistic as possible.

The result of the meeting was *Iggie's House*, Judy's first serious book for young people. It is about a Black family living in a white neighborhood. Judy wrote it because of a memory she had of when she was a little girl traveling on a train. All the Black people had to sit in the back seats. When she asked her mother why, her mother said it was because of segregation. At that time, Black people were not allowed to go to the same places or sit in the same areas as white people; they had to stay separated.

Judy started working on another book right away. She had the perfect idea for the kind of story that she would have liked to read when she was an adolescent. *Are You There God? It's Me, Margaret* is about a girl with lots of questions who feels that she can't really talk to her parents, so instead she talks to God. The book deals with important issues such as religion and what it's like to change from a girl into a young woman. Judy wrote the manuscript in just six weeks; because it was such

In 1981, Judy started a charity called The Kids Fund that donates money to organizations to help encourage communication between children and their parents. She also gives her time as a board member for other groups, such as the Society of Children's Book Writers and Illustrators, the Author's Guild, and the National Coalition Against Censorship (NCAC). The NCAC works to protect people's freedom of expression and thought and their right to question whatever they choose.

a personal story, the words came to her easily.

When *Margaret* was published in 1970, book critics loved it. Finally, Judy felt like a real writer that people took seriously. When Randy and Larry were in elementary school, Judy was so proud of her novel that she donated three copies to their school library. But to her shock, the librarian didn't put them on the shelf. When Judy asked why, she found out that the principal had banned the book, because the main character gets her first period. He thought children shouldn't be reading about puberty and menstruation, even though Judy argued that it was perfectly normal and natural.

> "The way to instill values in children is to talk about difficult issues, not restrict their access to books that may help them deal with their problems and concerns."
> — Judy Blume

Margaret became a bestseller, even though many groups tried to censor it (prevent people from reading it). One night, Judy's phone rang and the person on the line asked if she was the author of *"that book."* When Judy replied that yes, she was, the person yelled an insult into the phone and hung up. But negative comments didn't keep Judy from writing what she wanted to write.

Judy's characters came alive off the page. They were especially real to her because she spent all day with them creating their lives. When her children came home from school, Judy talked about the characters as though they were real people. "Guess what this character did today?" she'd ask Randy. Then she talked about what she'd written that day.

Over the next several years, Judy kept writing successful books. Some were about serious subjects. The book *It's Not the End of the World*, which came out in 1972, tells the story of a girl whose parents get divorced. *Blubber*, published in 1974, is about an overweight girl who is bullied by her classmates. Other books made readers laugh out loud, but Judy always made sure to include the characters' feelings about what happened to them, and not just make jokes. *Tales of a Fourth Grade Nothing* from 1972 and its follow-up book, *Superfudge* from 1980, share the ups and downs of a boy trying to cope with his impossible little brother.

Throughout her career, Judy has faced many problems with censorship, particularly during the 1970s and 1980s. While some librarians, teachers, parents, and critics have praised Judy's books for dealing with difficult issues — religion, sex, puberty, and relationships — in an honest way that children appreciate, many others have disagreed. Some people feel children ought to read novels that teach traditional values only. Because Judy's characters question religion and sex, and her stories don't always have happy endings, some worry that her books encourage young people to disobey their parents and ignore any good values they've been taught. But Judy's books do not really have that ef-

"I believe that censorship grows out of fear, and because fear is contagious, some parents are easily swayed. Book banning satisfies their need to feel in control of their children's lives … They want to believe that if their children don't read about it, their children won't know about it. And if they don't know about it, it won't happen."
— Judy Blume

fect on readers, and in the end, the decision over whether Judy's books are good or bad lies with the readers. Most of them are relieved that someone is willing to explore the questions some parents are too embarrassed to answer. They stand up for Judy because they love books that do not lie about how hard adolescence can be.

Judy is still very dedicated to speaking up against censorship. She feels strongly about the issue because of her own experiences with groups challenging her books. Many of her books have been banned in certain schools or libraries over the years. In 1999, Judy edited a collection of stories called *Places I Never Meant to Be: Original Stories by Censored Writers*. All the money earned from the book's sales goes to the National Coalition Against Censorship.

Judy started as a writer about forty years ago. She has written more than twenty books that millions of people continue to read and love. Every month, young readers write hundreds of letters to her. Many thank Judy for writing great stories and for understanding what it's like to face all the difficulties of growing up. Many tell her about their problems at school, at home, or with friends. Judy tries to answer as many letters as she can (she can't answer all of them, otherwise she'd never have time to write another book), and always encourages her readers to talk to their parents or to an adult they trust, something she wished she could have done as a young girl.

Like life, Judy Blume's books don't always have neat, perfect endings. She is brave enough to write about real problems that children face every day, and to describe what it's like to grow up with millions of questions and no answers. Even when so many people thought she was wrong, she wrote what was in her heart. Through rejection, tough criticism, and censorship, Judy never let other people stand in her way of writing the truth.

Margaret Atwood

1939 —

It takes a lot of hard work, but if you believe in yourself and you have an ambition to achieve a goal, you can make it happen. When Margaret Atwood was growing up, she was taught to believe that she could do anything. But often, even smart, talented women who work hard and believe in themselves have limitations imposed on them, and barriers placed in their way, simply because they are women. Margaret, however, overcame these obstacles, and forged an amazing career as a writer.

Just two months after the start of World War II, Margaret Eleanor Atwood was born on November 18, 1939, in

Ottawa, Ontario. Her upbringing was very different from that of many children. Her mother, also named Margaret (little Margaret was called Peggy so no one would get mixed up), was a nutritionist and her father, Carl, was an entomologist, a scientist who studies insects. Because of her father's job, Margaret's family spent a lot of time living in the bush of northern Ontario and Quebec. Sometimes they stayed in tents, other times they stayed in cabins that Carl built. They spent the warmer months in the bush, and lived in the city during the winter. They moved often, because Carl had to go to different areas for his research. Margaret's mother acted as her children's teacher when they lived too far from a school. For fun, she read books to them out loud.

Everybody had to pitch in, whether it was to prepare food, fetch firewood, or tidy up. The children were encouraged in whatever they did, and their parents always told them they were smart and capable. In the Atwood family, traditional roles for boys and girls didn't exist. Both Margaret and her brother Harold (he was two and a half years older than Margaret, and her sister Ruth was born in 1951) loved to play in the woods. Margaret was never squeamish about bugs or toads or snakes — wildlife was all around her. Sometimes Carl would spread out a big plastic sheet and catch insects on it. Margaret watched and learned as he studied them. Carl also taught his children the scientific names of every tree and plant, so they were always learning even when it wasn't time for lessons.

Margaret was rarely bored; she loved to paint and draw, and her parents taught her how to read very early.

Margaret Atwood

She began to write even before she knew how to spell the words correctly. She simply printed the words out the way they sounded. When she was five years old, she made her first book by cutting out the pages herself and sewing them together. Because Margaret loved cats, one book she wrote as a child was called *Rhyming Cats*. She also wrote plays and performed them with sock puppets.

In 1946, the Atwoods moved to Toronto when Carl took a job in the Zoology Department at the University of Toronto. Life was different, and Margaret didn't have as much freedom in the city as she did in the bush. But she liked going to the Royal Ontario Museum on Saturdays to see the mummies, or lying around reading comic books with Harold. She joined the Brownies, where she earned badges for doing crafts and learning ways to survive in the wilderness, but Margaret probably knew more about the outdoors than her group leaders did.

Margaret began high school in 1952, at Leaside High School. Because she had skipped grade seven, she was a year younger than the other girls. Margaret quickly became involved in the school's activities, such as theater, the basketball team, and the school newspaper. She got excellent grades, and often wondered what she wanted to be when she grew up. One of her textbooks listed the careers that were open to girls. It said a girl could be a teacher, a nurse, a flight attendant, a secretary, or a home economist. Margaret couldn't understand why there seemed to be so few choices, when she'd grown up knowing that she could do whatever she wanted.

Margaret thought about many different careers. Perhaps she would be a fashion designer or a painter, because she enjoyed doing both of those things. But one day while walking home from school in 1956, Margaret realized what she really wanted to be. At that moment, Margaret felt as though a giant thumb came out of the sky and pressed down on the top of her head. Suddenly, she had the idea for a poem that she absolutely had to write down. She didn't know where it came from, or why she had the idea at that particular moment, but it was then that Margaret knew she wanted to be a writer.

Not everyone understood Margaret's passion for writing. When she told her friends at lunchtime that she wanted to be a writer, the table fell silent. How could Margaret be a writer when it wasn't on the list of jobs women could do? When she told a friend's mother about her ambition, the response was that it was a good idea, because at least she could do it at home, meaning between cleaning the house and raising children. That picture wasn't exactly what Margaret had in mind. She wanted to be a serious, professional writer. Her parents worried a bit, too. They knew it could be difficult to make a living as a writer, and they wanted Margaret to have a stable job.

After graduation, Margaret attended Victoria College at the University of Toronto to study English literature. One of her professors was Northrop Frye, a famous literary critic. She studied hard during the school months and worked during the summers as a camp counselor and as a waitress. Reading and studying literature inspired Margaret to keep writing poetry, and she wrote all the time.

She was also inspired by meeting other young poets. The Bohemian Embassy was a coffee house in Toronto that held poetry readings late at night, and Margaret would go to listen and sometimes read her own pieces.

Margaret graduated with her bachelor's degree in 1961. She had begun to publish some of her poems in magazines, but she wanted to publish a book. Every year, for about four years, Margaret put together a collection of her poetry and sent it to a publisher. Every year it was returned with a rejection letter. Taking matters into her own hands, Margaret published a book herself called *Double Persephone*, which was seven pages long. She sold the books for fifty cents each. Besides writing, Margaret decided to continue her education at Harvard University in Massachusetts, where she got her master's degree.

In 1963, Margaret went back to Toronto hoping to work for a while, because in school she hadn't had time to do much else besides studying, and so she was out of money. She worked for a market research company called Canadian Facts. It wasn't her dream job, but outside of work she began to

Margaret Atwood in 1967.

write a novel. Margaret stored her experiences at the company in the back of her mind. As a writer, she looked at every experience — good or bad — as something she might write about some day. She then moved to Vancouver and lived there for a few years, teaching a grammar course and writing poetry.

In 1966, Contact Press published Margaret's first book of poetry, called *The Circle Game*. She was back at Harvard, studying to get her doctorate. Although Margaret did well at university, she knew that all she really wanted to do was be a writer, and do her own work rather than studying other writers all day long. The encouragement she needed came in 1967, when *The Circle Game* was nominated for a Governor General's Award (G.G.), the biggest Canadian literary award at the time. Because she didn't usually dress up, Margaret had to borrow a dress and shoes from her friends to wear at the award ceremony in Ottawa. She never expected to win such a major award, but at 27 years old she became the youngest person to win the G.G.

Margaret's career was on a good path, and her dream of becoming a full-time writer was coming true.

Margaret's books are copyrighted under the name O.W. Toad, which is also the domain name for her website. It's an anagram (meaning the letters of one word are rearranged to make a new word) for her last name, Atwood.

Next, her first novel, *The Edible Woman*, was published by McClelland and Stewart to very good reviews. In the novel, the main character, Marian, feels smothered by her job at a market research company and by her fiancé. The book deals with ideas of what society thinks women should be, versus what each woman wants to be. Of course, a successful novel doesn't guarantee glamour for the author: Margaret's first book signing took place at the Hudson's Bay Company store in Edmonton, Alberta in 1967, in the men's sock and underwear department!

Around 1970, Margaret attended a party hosted by Milton Acorn, a poet from Charlottetown. There she met a writer named Graeme Gibson who had been nominated for the G.G. that year. Margaret told Graeme she thought his book should have won, and they started a conversation. Over the course of a few years, they began seeing more and more of each other, became very close, and eventually moved in together. In 1976, their daughter, Jess, was born.

Although Margaret's reputation as a fine writer was growing, she still needed to do other work to support herself. She took a position as an assistant professor at York University in the English Department. At the same time, Margaret was an editor at House of Anansi Press, a small publisher in Toronto, which was founded by two writers, Dennis Lee and Dave Godfrey. She read manuscripts and helped to decide which should be published and how to improve them. Another job she held was more unusual — Margaret got to use her love of drawing to create a regular comic strip for *This Magazine* entitled "Kanadian Kulture Komics."

By the 1980s, Margaret was able to write full time, just as she had always dreamed of doing. She wrote daring books, and many people looked up to her as a great writer and a feminist. One of her best-known works from 1985 is called *The Handmaid's Tale*. It is a novel set in the future in which there is almost no freedom, especially for women. The novel became an international success and gave Margaret, and Canadian literature, great exposure.

High school and university students in countries around the world study *The Handmaid's Tale* in class. However, Margaret doesn't just write books for adults, she writes children's stories as well. Like her books for grown-ups, these stories give children something to think about and they're enjoyable to read. You can see Margaret's sense of humor and love of language in the titles alone, such as *Princess Prunella and the Purple Peanut*, *Rude Ramsey and the Roaring Radishes*, and *Bashful Bob and Doleful Dorinda*.

Not just an author but an activist, too, Margaret recognized that as a well-known writer, she wanted to help bring people's attention toward important causes. She held the position of president of the Canadian section of PEN International for two years. PEN is an organization that defends free speech and works to free writers who are imprisoned for what they write.

Speaking about how she felt as a women writer in the 1960s, Margaret said: "I feared rejection as a lady writer … and I was convinced that I would never get married. The biographies of women authors were very clear: you could write and be classified as neurotic or you could get married and be fulfilled. Being fulfilled sounded very dull."

In 2000, Margaret was entrusted to help make an important decision as a member of the jury for the Giller Prize. Four years earlier, Margaret had won the award (a top prize in Canadian literature) for her novel *Alias Grace*, based on true events about Grace Marks, a woman accused of murder in

Margaret Atwood

the 1800s. Along with her co-judges, writers Alistair MacLeod and Jane Urquhart, Margaret had to choose which book would win. Many talented authors were nominated and the decision proved to be impossible. It is the only time since the prize began in 1994 that the Giller has been was awarded to two authors at once.

Margaret Atwood in 1988.

Besides helping to award prizes to other writers, Margaret has won many prizes for her own writing. That same year, her novel *The Blind Assassin* won the prestigious Booker Prize (now the Man Booker Prize), for the best novel of the year written by a citizen of the British Commonwealth. Although she was nominated for the award for three previous novels (*The Handmaid's Tale*, *Cat's Eye*, and *Alias Grace*) this was the first time she had won.

As a busy international author, Margaret has been on many book tours in her career. They are often exhausting, with schedules that barely allow her time to eat or sleep. Margaret wondered if she could find a way to make things easier. She invented the LongPen machine, which launched in 2006. The author signs her autographs on

In an interview with the CBC in 2000, Margaret was asked if she worried about people saying negative things about her work. She said, "Some people aren't going to like you, and there are some people who aren't going to like what you do, no matter what it is. So why not have fun and do what you want?"

a computer pad. The computer pad transmits the signature to a robotic arm holding a pen, which can be anywhere else in the world. The arm recreates the signature just as the author wrote, and fans can even talk with the author using a webcam, and keep a DVD of the conversation as a souvenir. Many people thought that it didn't make sense for a writer to become an inventor, but Margaret thought it made perfect sense. The way she put it, a writer is a kind of inventor, who creates things (such as stories and characters) out of words.

Some critics and scholars spend a lot of time trying to figure Margaret out. Surely a person who writes so incredibly must have deep dark secrets, or lead a very complicated life. While Margaret will certainly discuss her work, she refuses to explain herself as a writer or as a person. She lets the books speak for themselves.

Margaret makes her home in Toronto. Her latest book, from 2006, is called *The Tent*, a collection of witty essays accompanied by Margaret's own illustrations. She has written more than forty books, including poetry and literary criticism, as well as too many magazine articles and essays to count. She is never afraid to challenge herself as a writer, and explores diverse topics, from politics to science fiction. Her work just keeps getting better and fans around the world are always eager to read what she will write next.

J.K. Rowling

1965 —

It takes lots of hard work to make a life dream come true. All kinds of obstacles can stand in our way, from family problems, money problems, or even that feeling that maybe we just can't do it. J.K. Rowling is one writer who faced difficulties just like these, but overcame them to become one of the most famous children's authors in the world today. What was her secret? She refused to let anything distract her from her passion for writing.

Anne and Peter Rowling (pronounced ROLLING) got married when they were both 19 years old. The next year, on July 31, 1965, their first daughter, Joanne, was born, and they called her Jo for short. The family lived in the small town of Chipping Sodbury, which is outside of London, England. Two years later, they had another daughter and named her Dianne, and they called her Di for short.

Like most sisters, the Rowling girls had their share of squabbles, but they were also best friends. Their parents loved books and read to Jo and Di often. Jo thought the best stories were the ones that involved lots of imagination, such as *The Wind In the Willows*, in which animals talk just like people do. Books such as this captured Jo's already wild imagination, and she began to make up her own stories and create her own worlds where anything might happen. She especially liked one character she invented, a rabbit named Rabbit. Sometimes, the girls turned the stories into plays and acted out the different parts.

During their early childhood, the Rowling girls lived in a neighborhood with lots of other children, among them a brother and sister named Ian and Vikki Potter. (Years later, Jo remembered she liked their last name and used it for her famous character, Harry Potter.)

School took up a lot of time, too, but Jo didn't mind studying, especially if it was for her favorite class, English. The books she read growing up inspired her to keep writing stories about strong, smart children. When she read *Little Women* by Louisa May Alcott, Jo identified strongly with the main character Jo, not just because they shared a name, but because they also had similar personality traits — both were good at school and always believed in putting family first.

In 1974 the Rowlings moved to Tuthill, another small town. Their new house was located next to a graveyard, which many people thought was creepy — but not Jo. She approached it the way a writer would, and sometimes walked there, imagining what each person's life had been like.

The "K" in J.K. Rowling stands for Kathleen. It is the name of Jo's grandmother, who died in 1973. Just before her first book was published, Jo took on the initial to pay tribute to her grandmother, and her name appears this way on the covers of all of her books.

In the new town, Jo was nervous about her new school, where the students wore uniforms, and she wondered if she would make friends. She was right to be a bit nervous, because from the start, she had to prove herself. One of her teachers was really tough on the class. In fact, the teacher even sat the students in order of how good their grades were, so those with the highest marks sat on one side of the room and those with the lowest marks sat on the other side. Right away, Jo sat on the side for students with low marks, because she did poorly on a math test. Jo didn't think it was fair to make people feel bad just because they didn't have the best grades. Math was difficult for her, but she had a talent for writing, and other students had their own strengths as well. Jo was determined to prove that she couldn't be classified based on just one thing. She studied math every night and was eventually moved to the other side of the class.

One day, when Jo was 15 years old, she noticed that her mother had trouble lifting a teapot, something she did every day. It turned out that her mother had multiple sclerosis, a disease that affects a person's central nervous system and makes it hard for them to control their muscles. At first, Jo didn't want to believe that her strong, smart mother was sick, but eventually she had to accept it. Although Anne's body was weak, she kept up her spirits and tried to stay positive for her children, something Jo admired.

After graduating from high school in 1983, Jo went to the University of Exeter. It wasn't too far from her family, so she took the train home on the weekends. Although English was her passion, Jo's parents insisted that she study different subjects such as French and Greek and Roman studies. Wanting to please them, she did. She graduated, but felt the whole time she was studying that her heart wasn't in it. So she continued to write stories and lose herself in her imagination. Jo knew she wanted to be a writer.

A writer's life can be difficult. Because many of them don't make a lot of money, they have to work at other jobs to pay for rent and food. Jo worked as a secretary to earn her living. Spending all day in an office typing things other people wrote didn't suit her at all. She wanted to develop her own writing skills. But Jo found a way around the daily boredom. Every day at lunch, she left the office and found a quiet place to sit and write short stories. Sometimes, she lost track of time and came back late because she was so involved in her own work.

Jo often wrote stories for adults, but out of nowhere the idea for a children's book came to her, when she was riding on a train in 1990. It would be about a young wizard named Harry Potter, and although he had magic powers, he would be a lot like regular children. Immediately, Jo had so many ideas she was afraid she would forget them. For once, she didn't have a pen to write them all down. But luckily, there was a problem with the train that day, and all the passengers had to wait four hours. Normally, waiting can be boring, but Jo used that time to figure out what would happen to Harry, who his friends would be and what kind of world he would live in. As soon as she got her hands on a pen and paper when she got home, Jo began to write.

With a fun, exciting writing project to work on, things were going well for Jo. She loved creating a fantasy-filled world, where she made her dreams real simply by writing them down. She had more and more pages every day, and was very happy until December of that same year, when her mother died.

Jo had never felt so sad in her life. To deal with her mother's death, she knew she had to get away from England for a while. She moved to Portugal and began teaching English classes in the afternoons and the evenings. The schedule suited her perfectly, because during the day she had time to work on the story of Harry Potter. Writing about him helped to cheer her up, and she knew her mother would be proud if someday the book got published. Jo also met a man in Portugal whom she married in 1992. One of the best days of her life came when she had a baby girl, Jessica, the following year. The marriage ended when Jessica was still a baby, so in 1994 Jo took her daughter away from Portugal to Edinburgh, Scotland, where her sister Di lived.

It was a stressful time. Jo had no job and very little money. For a short while, she had to go on social assistance, which is a government program that gives financial help to those who need it. Even her greatest passion, writing, was a problem. She even felt guilty for doing it because writing didn't pay the bills. Jo wondered if writing was worth doing at all, if she couldn't support herself and her daughter. But every time she picked up a pen and saw the story growing, she knew that some dreams should never be put aside.

Determined to make a living, Jo went to school to get her Scottish teaching certificate and graduated with straight As. She got a teaching job and began the routine of being a mother, writer, and teacher. At times it felt like the manuscript would never be finished. Jo could write only when Jessica was asleep, so as soon as the baby closed her eyes, Jo wheeled her to a coffee shop in her stroller and wrote as much as she could. She wrote by hand, on pads of paper, scribbling away as fast as her hand would allow. When the baby woke up, writing time was over.

Jo spent a lot of time planning out the elements of the book — details are very important to her. She even had the plot worked out for all seven books in the series before they were written! To help make her characters as real as possible, Jo made notes about each one. She wrote their biographies, decided what they like and don't like, and what they might say in given situation. She even made sketches of what the characters should look like. She worked every day, and finally finished the manuscript for *Harry Potter and the Philosopher's Stone* (or *Harry Potter and the Sorcerer's Stone*, the title under which it was published in the U.S.) in 1995.

But the hard part wasn't over. Like most writers, Jo worried that no publisher would like her manuscript and she felt some doubt about whether or not to send it out. To conquer her fear, Jo thought about how having people read it and not like it was better than no one ever reading it at all. She had to take a chance, and she sent the manuscript to a literary agent named Christopher Little. An agent's job is to take an unpublished manuscript to different publishers, to convince them that they should publish the book. After a year of rejection, Jo got an important phone call in August 1996. Her book was going to be published!

> Although Jo's books are loved by millions of children and adults all over the world, it doesn't mean everyone embraces Harry Potter's adventures. In fact, some groups have tried to ban the books because they think children shouldn't read about wizards and magic. It may sound strange to those who love her writing, but Jo is actually number four on the American Library Association's list of authors whose work people tried to ban from 1999 to 2004.

After the first Harry Potter book came out in the United Kingdom in 1997, word spread quickly that it was a truly incredible book, and it came out in North America soon after. Suddenly, Jo found herself the center of attention of readers all over the world. Although she was glad that she didn't have to work as a secretary any more, it took Jo some time to get used to being famous. Reporters wanted to interview her and fans wrote her lots of letters. She gave

Jo at a *Harry Potter* book signing.

book signings and readings and saw her picture in magazines and newspapers, even on television.

Some people let success change them, but not Jo. When she began making money, one of the first things she bought was a house, where she could have a space in which to write more about Harry Potter. Because readers were so excited about the first book, Jo wrote the next ones very quickly. *Harry Potter and the Chamber of Secrets* was published in 1998, *Harry Potter and the Prisoner of Azkaban* in 1999.

Not many authors become celebrities, but Jo's fame could never be questioned after an event at the SkyDome stadium in Toronto in the year 2000. There, Jo gave one of the biggest public book readings ever, to a crowd of over 12,000 people who gathered to hear her read from *Harry*

Potter and the Goblet of Fire. Normally such a big venue is a place where rock stars perform, and Jo was shaking at first — she'd never had such a huge audience before. After the applause died down, she said "Thank you. I am delighted and terrified to be here." Then, in March of 2001, the Queen of England herself honored Jo with an Order of the British Empire, a medal that is only given to British citizens of remarkable achievement.

Life just got busier. Jo married Dr. Neil Murray, an anesthesiologist, on December 26, 2001. Then, the motion picture company Warner Brothers released *Harry Potter and the Philosopher's Stone* as a movie, and afterwards wanted to make all the following books into movies too. Jo made sure she got to help with the script and give her approval. As the creator of the stories, she wanted the movie

A collection of the Harry Potter books by J.K. Rowling.

to be just right, so children who saw it wouldn't be disappointed.

A big year for Jo was 2003. First, the fifth Harry Potter book was published that summer, *Harry Potter and the Order of the Phoenix.* Her fans all over the world were so eager to read about what would happen next to their favorite hero, the book sold millions of copies its first day in stores. Second, Jo became a mother again.

> "I am an extraordinarily lucky person, doing what I love best in the world. I'm sure that I will always be a writer. It was wonderful enough just to be published. The greatest reward is the enthusiasm of the readers."
> — J.K. Rowling

She gave birth to a baby boy, whom she named David. Her third child, a daughter named Mackenzie, was born in 2005, which thrilled Jo because she'd always dreamed of having three children.

Jo still manages to take time out of her whirlwind life to do things that are important to her, such as charity work. She is very outspoken on the subject of human rights for children and has helped to raise money and awareness for the cause. She wrote two short books about the world of Harry and donated the profits to Comic Relief, a British organization that helps the poor. Jo also donates her money and time to groups who work to find a cure for multiple sclerosis, in honor of her mother.

Jo's most recent book, the sixth in the series, is *Harry Potter and the Half-Blood Prince,* which was published in 2005. Readers everywhere are excited to read the seventh and final book in the series and can hardly wait to find out what happens. You can read rumors in newspapers and on the internet about how it will all end and what the title will be, but Jo is very good at keeping a secret. She wants readers to enjoy the book when they read it and doesn't want to spoil their fun.

Jo's books help children around the world to let their imaginations run wild. They have sold millions of copies and have been translated into more than sixty languages. But the idea of fame, money, and adoring readers was not what inspired her to write when she was tired, when she had little money, or when she thought she should give up. It was her love of writing that kept her going. To show this point in an interview, J.K. Rowling once said: "I love writing these books. I don't think anyone could enjoy reading them more than I enjoy writing them."

Sources

Jane Austen

Laski, Marghanita. *Jane Austen and Her World*. New York: Charles Scribner's Sons, 1975.

Le Faye, Deirdre. *Jane Austen*. New York: Oxford University Press, 1998.

Jane Austen's Life. American Home Treasures Inc., 1997 (video).

Presumption: Life of Jane Austen. BBC Worldwide Americas, 1995 (video).

www.jane-austens-house-museum.org.uk/   (Jane Austen's House)

www.austen.com   (A website dedicated to Jane Austen)

http://www.hants.gov.uk/austen/chawton.html   (Hampshire City Council Website: Jane Austen Page)

Harriet Beecher Stowe

Ash, Maureen. *The Story of Harriet Beecher Stowe*. Chicago: Children's Press, 1990.

Fritz, Jean. *Harriet Beecher Stowe and the Beecher Preachers*. New York: Penguin Putnam Books for Young Readers. 1994.

Johnston, Norma. Harriet: The Life and World of Harriet Beecher Stowe. New York: Beech Tree. 1990.

Harriet (Elizabeth) Beecher Stowe. *Contemporary Authors Online*. Gale, 2003.

www.harrietbeecherstowecenter.org   (The Harriet Beecher Stowe Center)

George Eliot

Brady, Kristin. *Women Writers: George Eliot*. London: MacMillan Education Ltd, 1992.

Grenier, Cynthia. "Passion and Ideas: A Profile of George Eliot," in *World and I*. October 2003, v. 18, p. 250.

Nadel, Ira B., and Fredeman, William E., (eds). "George Eliot," in *Dictionary of Literary Biography, Volume 21: Victorian Novelists Before 1885.* Vancouver: Bruccoli Clark Layman Book. The Gale Group, 1983, pp. 145–170.

Uglow, Jennifer. *George Eliot.* London: Virago Press Ltd, 1987.

Louisa May Alcott

Delamar, Gloria T. *Louisa May Alcott and "Little Women."* Jefferson: McFarland & Company Inc., 1990.

Gormley, Beatrice. *Louisa May Alcott: Young Novelist.* New York: Aladdin Paperbacks, 1999.

Silverthorne, Elizabeth. *Louisa May Alcott.* Philadelphia: Chelsea House Publishers, 2002.

www.louisamayalcott.org/index.html   (Orchard House: Home of the Alcotts)

Lucy Maud Montgomery

Andronik, Catherine M. *Kindred Spirit: A Biography of L.M. Montgomery, Creator of Anne of Green Gables.* New York: MacMillan Publishing Company, 1996.

New, W. H. (ed). *Dictionary of Literary Biography,* Volume 92: Canadian Writers, 1890–1920. A Bruccoli Clark Layman Book. University of British Columbia. The Gale Group, 1990, pp. 246-253.

Innis, Mary Quayle. *The Clear Spirit: Twenty Canadian Women and their Times.* Toronto: University of Toronto Press, 1967.

Rubio, Mary and Waterson, Elizabeth. *Writing a Life: L.M. Montgomery.* Toronto: ECW Press, 1995.

www.upei.ca/~lmmi/   (L.M. Montgomery Institute)

www.gov.pe.ca/lmm/index.php3   (Prince Edward Island's provincial website)

Toni Morrison

Century, Douglas. *Toni Morrison: Author.* New York: Chelsea House Publishers, 1994.

Toni Morrison. Home Vision, 1987 (video).

http://www.kirjasto.sci.fi/tmorris.htm   (A biography of Toni Morrison)

www.nobelprize.org   (Toni Morrison's Nobel Lecture)

Sources

www.salon.com/books/int/1998/02/cov%5Fsi%5F02int.html   (Salon.com interview with Toni Morrison)

Joy Kogawa

Harris, Mason. *Joy Kogawa and Her Works.* Toronto: ECW Press, 1998.

Silvera, Makeda. (Ed.) *The Other Woman: Women of Colour in Contemporary Canadian Literature.* "Heart-of- the-Matter Questions." Interview with Joy Kogawa by Karlyn Koh. Toronto: Sister Vision Press, 1995.

Williamson, Janice. *Sounding Differences: Conversations with Seventeen Canadian Women Writers.* Toronto: University of Toronto Press, 1993.

June Callwood's National Treasures Series: Joy Kogawa. Vision. Magic Lantern Communications Inc. (Video) 1998.

B.C. BookWorld Author Bank
www.abcbookworld.com

www.kogawahouse.com

www.kogawa.homestead.com

National Association of Japanese Canadians
www.najc.ca

Judy Blume

Blume, Judy. *Letters to Judy: What Your Kids Wish They Could Tell You.* New York: G.P. Putnam's Sons, 1986.

Lee, Betsy. *Judy Blume's Story.* Toronto: Scholastic Book Services, 1981.

Wheeler, Jill C. *Judy Blume.* Abdo & Daughters: Edina, Minnesota, 1996.

"Judy Blume," in *Dictionary of Literary Biography*, Volume 52: American Writers for Children Since 1960: Fiction. Bruccoli Clark Layman Book. The Gale Group, 1986, pp. 30–38.

www.judyblume.com   (Judy Blume's Home Base)

www.cnn.com/books/beginnings/9908/places.never/ ("Fighting Back Against Censorship")

Margaret Atwood

Atwood, Margaret. "Why I Write Poetry." *This Magazine.* March/April, 1996.

Ingersoll, Earl G. *Margaret Atwood: Conversations.* Willowdale: Firefly Books Ltd., 1990.

Keller, Julia. "A Writer Writ Large." *The Chicago Tribune.* October 30, 2005.

Pacienza, Angela. "Author-turned-inventor Margaret Atwood launches book-signing gadget Canadian Press." The Canadian Press. Feb 28, 2006.

Potts, Robert. "Light in the Wilderness." *The Guardian.* April 26, 2003.

Sullivan, Rosemary. *The Red Shoes: Margaret Atwood Starting Out.* Toronto: HaperCollins Canada, 1998.

Margaret Atwood: Once in August. Video. National Film Board of Canada. 1984

CBC Archives: Margaret Atwood
http://archives.cbc.ca/IDD-1-68-1494/arts_entertainment/margaret_atwood

Margaret Atwood Information Site
www.owtoad.com

J.K. Rowling

Clark, Connie Ann. *J.K. Rowling: A Biography.* Westport: Greenwood Press, 2003.

Compson, William. *J.K. Rowling.* New York: The Rosen Publishing Group, Inc., 2003.

Shapiro, Marc. *J.K. Rowling: The Wizard Behind Harry Potter.* New York: St. Martins Griffin, 2004.

www.jkrowling.com   (J.K. Rowling Official Site)

www.mugglenet.com

http://www.the-leaky-cauldron.org

www.scholastic.com/harrypotter/author/

Photo Credits

Front Cover

Margaret Atwood: photo courtesy Jim Allen

Lucy Maud Montgomery: Canadian Heritage Gallery

J.K. Rowling: photo by Gorden Wright

Joy Kogawa: photo courtesy John Flanders

Judy Blume: photo courtesy Sigrid Estrada

Jane Austen

page 9: photo courtesy Project Gutenburg

page 13: photo courtesy Project Gutenburg

Harriet Beecher Stowe

page 19: Library of Congress Prints and Photographs Division Washington, D.C. 20540 USA, LC-USZ62-11212

page 26: Library of Congress Prints and Photographs Division Washington, D.C. 20540 USA, LC-USZ62-10476

George Eliot

all images public domain

Louisa May Alcott

page 41: Library of Congress Prints and Photographs Division Washington, D.C. 20540 USA, LC-USZ61-452

page 46: photo courtesy the Concord Free Public Library

Lucy Maud Montgomery

Toni Morrison

Joy Kogawa

Judy Blume

Margaret Atwood

J.K. Rowling